Building The Frick Collection

Henry Clay Frick and his granddaughter Adelaide at Eagle Rock, Frick's summer home in Pride's Crossing, Massachusetts, 1919.

Building The Frick Collection

An Introduction to the House and Its Collections

Colin B. Bailey

The Frick Collection, New York
In association with Scala Arts Publishers

SCALA

Text and Photography Copyright © 2006 The Frick Collection

Published by
The Frick Collection
1 East 70th Street
New York, NY 10021
www.frick.org

In association with
Scala Arts Publishers, Inc.
1301 Avenue of the Americas, 10th Floor
New York, NY 10019
www.scalapublishers.com

First published in 2006

Distributed in the booktrade by
ACC Publishing Group
6 West 18th Street, Suite 4B
New York, NY 10011
United States of America

Library of Congress Cataloguing-in-Publication Data available
upon request.

ISBN: 978 1 85759 381 5 (hardback)
ISBN: 978 0 912114 30 9 (paperback)

This publication was organized at The Frick Collection by
Elaine Koss, Editor in Chief; Margaret Iacono, Assistant
Curator; Mary Lydecker, Administrative Assistant to the
Curatorial Department

For Scala Arts Publishers, Inc.:
Design: Pooja Bakri
Project Manager: Kate Norment
Commissioning Editor: Jennifer Wright
Production Manager: Claudia Varosio
Index: Joan Dearnley

Produced by Scala Arts Publishers, Inc.
Printed and bound in China

10 9 8 7 6

Reprinted in 2018

Contents

Preface and Acknowledgments

Although there have been several books devoted to Henry Clay Frick and The Frick Collection, none as yet has sought to document the building at 1 East 70th Street and to see how the creation of this residence influenced the taste of the collector in the final years of his life. And while the additions to Thomas Hastings's original mansion and the acquisitions made after Frick's death are known to specialists, the general public is still poorly informed about the history of The Frick Collection and its growth in the decades following the collector's death. Using material from the institutional archives of The Frick Collection and Frick family papers—recently deposited at the Frick Art Reference Library by the Helen Clay Frick Foundation—which contain floor plans, elevations, photographs, and drawings in the holdings of The Frick Collection, I have tried to document the history of the house and its owner, chronicling the various stages of the planning, construction, and installation of Frick's residence at 1 East 70th Street. Through newly discovered letters and telegrams, Frick's passionate and demanding involvement in the project is revealed for the first time, as are the roles of the various dealers, architects, decorators, and fellow collectors who advised him. Most of the photographs used in the book belong to The Frick Collection and were taken by staff photographers or contracted photographers over the years. The blueprints and plans reproduced here likewise belong primarily to The Frick Collection. The work on preparing these for reproduction has been done by the Conservation Department of the Frick Art Reference Library.

I am greatly indebted to previous biographies of Henry Clay Frick as well as to the many recent studies of domestic architecture and interior decoration in New York and Pittsburgh during the Gilded Age; these are listed in the Select Bibliography at the end of the book. The early sections of this study set Frick's achievement in context and throw new light on the roles played by Thomas Hastings, Elsie de Wolfe, and Sir Charles Allom in the building and furnishing of 1 East 70th Street. The section devoted to John Russell Pope's extension of the original mansion between 1931 and 1935 introduces a wealth of little-known period installation photography and also covers the creation of the Frick Art Reference Library. A final section surveys the additions to the Collection and the building campaign of 1973–77, whose most important component was the creation of Russell Page's 70th Street Garden.

It is a pleasure to acknowledge the many friends, colleagues, and specialists who have assisted me in the writing of this book. Above all, I wish to thank Yvonne H. Elet, The Frick's first Mellon Fellow and a superb architectural historian specializing in an earlier period, who mapped out the territory to be considered with remarkable thoroughness and aplomb; and Margaret Iacono, Associate Research Curator of The Frick Collection, whose meticulous research into each of the sections of this book made it possible for me to write this text in a relatively short period of time. Colleagues at the Frick Art Reference Library could not have been more generous or more careful in reviewing material, creating new photography, and making available the deep resources of the Frick family archive: I am most grateful to Patricia Barnett, Don Swanson, Sally Brazil, Julie Ludwig, and Susan Chore. At The Frick Collection, the contributions of Mary Lydecker and Michael Bodycomb have been immense, and I am truly thankful for the sensitive editing of Elaine Koss, former Editor in Chief, who has also supervised all aspects of the design and production of this book. Former Director Anne L. Poulet shared her research into Frick as a collector of the decorative arts with me, and Galen Lee, Horticulturalist at The Frick Collection, generously allowed me to read his unpublished manuscript, "Gardens of the Frick Collection from Olmsted to Russell Page," and answered many questions. At Scala Publishers, I want to acknowledge Jennifer Wright, whose idea for a short book on the Frick led to this expanded version; Kate Norment, who coordinated the production of the book for Scala; and Pooja Bakri, who is responsible for the elegant design. Two eminent scholars of this period, Edgar Munhall, Curator Emeritus, The Frick Collection, and DeCourcy McIntosh, doyen of Pittsburgh and the Gilded Age, both gave earlier drafts of my text a close reading and made very helpful suggestions. I would also like to acknowledge the assistance of Christopher Gray and Michael C. Kathrens.

Colin B. Bailey

Prologue

The history of the building at 1 East 70th Street that houses The Frick Collection—designed by Thomas Hastings in 1912–13, transformed by John Russell Pope between 1932 and 1935, and extended for a second time between 1973 and 1977—is part architectural study, part family biography, part institutional record. The conception, planning, and erection of Hastings's Indiana limestone mansion were intimately connected to Henry Clay Frick's ambitions as a collector. From the very beginning, the house was intended to serve as a museum—after the deaths of the founder and his wife—"for the use and benefit of all persons whomsoever." During their lifetime, it was to provide the setting for Frick's incomparable collection of old masters and nineteenth-century paintings. But the house was also a home—to Frick, his wife, Adelaide, his daughter Helen Clay (less so his son, Childs), and some twenty-seven servants. After construction ended and the interiors began to take shape, Frick became more keenly aware of how sculpture, furniture, and the decorative arts in general might enhance the rooms and halls in which his pictures hung. Gradually, the same discrimination and insistence on quality that had long marked his activity as a collector of paintings were applied to his selection of objects for the furnishing of the major ground-floor rooms. In this regard, the death of J. Pierpont Morgan in Rome in March 1913 and the display of his enormous collection in a memorial exhibition at The Metropolitan Museum of Art between February 1914 and May 1916 had an enormous impact on Frick's taste and the completion of his house. Thanks to the English art dealer Joseph Duveen, in 1915 and 1916 Frick acquired many of the finest objects from Morgan's collection—a suite of paintings by Fragonard, Limoges enamels, Renaissance bronzes, Sèvres porcelains, eighteenth-century French furniture—thus establishing the various specializations (in addition to paintings) for which The Frick Collection has been renowned since it opened to the public in December 1935.

By focusing on the building of The Frick Collection (and, to a lesser extent, the Frick Art Reference Library), this architectural survey contributes also to our understanding of the founder (and his daughter) in their roles as clients, patrons, and collectors. When one maps the sometimes painful progress in the construction and furnishing of 1 East 70th Street, the force of Frick's personality, and his likes and dislikes, emerges with a clarity he most certainly would have found distasteful. It is well known that this notoriously taciturn collector left scant record of his opinions on the works of art he so voraciously acquired. A further objective of this study has been to identify and evaluate the contributions of those who advised and encouraged Frick as a builder and a collector. All too often, his achievement has been understood as a supremely personal undertaking; the abundant documentation, however, suggests that Frick was keenly attentive to the opinions and actions of trusted advisers, dealers, and fellow collectors.

I. Origins in Pittsburgh

Henry Clay Frick was born on 19 December 1849, in West Overton, Westmoreland County, Pennsylvania, some forty miles southeast of Pittsburgh (fig. 1). He was the oldest son (and the second of six children) of John W. Frick, a less than enterprising farmer, and Elizabeth Overholt, daughter of an industrious and prosperous whiskey distiller, who left an estate valued at $400,000 at his death in January 1870. Frick received little formal education: "So badly were my services needed in the earning of the family living that I was allowed to go to school only in the winter months." From modest Mennonite stock—Andrew Carnegie claimed, in error, that he had started his career as a "poor railway clerk"—Frick worked as a salesman in one of Pittsburgh's most prominent stores and became the well-paid chief bookkeeper for the family distillery at Broadford (he retained an expertise in accounting for the rest of his life).

West Overton was also eight miles north of Connellsville, a center in the fledgling coke industry, whose rich coal beds yielded seams of high-grade bituminous coal, ideal for coking. In March 1871 Frick, in partnership with a cousin, invested family money to acquire low-priced coking fields and build fifty coke ovens. Within a decade, H. C. Frick Coke Company would operate some thousand working ovens and produce almost 80 percent of the coke used by Pittsburgh's iron and steel industries—coke being the essential fuel needed in the smelting of iron ore, which was required in ever-greater quantities for the creation of steel. Frick owned his first company at twenty-two, earned his first million by the age of thirty, and entered into partnership with the steel manufacturer Andrew Carnegie (1835–1919) in May 1882. For the next two decades, as the expansion of the railways created an ever-increasing demand for iron and steel (the leading industries in America by the eve of the First World War), Frick dedicated himself wholeheartedly to the joint fortunes of the H. C. Frick Coke Company and Carnegie Brothers & Company. When these two entities merged in 1892, Frick was appointed chairman of Carnegie Steel Co., Ltd., capitalized at $25 million and employing some 30,000 men.

Even as a young man, Frick was interested in pictures. An officer from the newly founded Mellon Bank, sent from Pittsburgh to Broadford in 1870 to assess Frick's suitability for a second loan of $10,000, noted that he lived surrounded by prints and sketches, "some made by himself and all out of place in this half office and half living room in a clapboard shack." Frick's request to the bank was rejected, but for a second opinion Mellon sent a more open-minded mining partner, who granted the loan—though he noted that the applicant "may be a little too enthusiastic about pictures, but not

1   Henry Clay Frick as a young man, 1880.   2   Frick and Adela de Childs Frick in Boston on their honeymoon, 1882.

enough to hurt." Once launched in the coke industry, Frick moved to Pittsburgh, renting rooms in the Monongahela House in 1880 and establishing residence in the prosperous Homewood section of the city after his marriage in December 1881 to Adelaide Howard Childs (1859–1931), daughter of a boot and shoe manufacturer (fig. 2). Frick's first home was an eleven-room, two-and-a-half-story house purchased for $25,000 in August 1882 and renovated by a Scottish architect, Andrew Peebles, for double that amount. (Frick and his wife took occupancy six months later.) This Italianate house, called Clayton, was remodeled in 1892 by the twenty-six-year-old architect Frederick Osterling, who transformed it into a twenty-three-room four-story Loire château (fig. 3)—a style popularized during the 1870s in New York by Richard Morris Hunt, architect of the Lenox Library. Clayton's interiors were designed by Osterling in part in high Victorian, Eastlake style, with many of the furnishings coming from New York firms (A. Kimbel & Sons, D. Hess & Co, and Knoedler's). The rooms served

3   Frick purchased Clayton for $25,000 in 1882. It is now part of the Frick Art and Historical Center in Pittsburgh.

4   F. Roset , *Portrait of Mrs. Henry Clay Frick and Children*, 1889. Property of Henry Clay Frick II, on loan to the Frick Art and Historical Center.

as a setting for Frick's modest collection of family portraits (fig. 4) and modern landscapes and genre paintings by minor local and international artists, typical of those found in the homes of the Pittsburgh elite.

It was only after Frick tendered his resignation to Carnegie Steel Co., Ltd., in December 1894 and was appointed chairman of the board that his activities as a collector gained purpose and direction. His friendship with the dealer Roland Knoedler (1856–1932) dates from the second half of the 1890s, and between 1895 and 1900 Frick acquired more than ninety pictures. Once again, these were nearly all modern works, but now by fashionable (and expensive) Parisian Salon artists such as Bouguereau, Breton, and Gérôme, whose studios Frick visited, in Knoedler's company, during their summer trips to Paris. (Frick also bought an Impressionist landscape by Monet in 1895.) Frick was particularly taken by Cazin and Dagnan-Bouveret: from the latter he commissioned in 1898 a portrait

5   The dining room at Clayton with Pascal-Adolphe-Jean Dagnan-Bouveret's *Consolatrix Afflictorum*, 1899.
     Frick Art and Historical Center.

of his son, Childs, as well as the mournful *Consolatrix Afflictorum* for the dining room at Clayton (fig. 5). (The Fricks had lost their five-year-old daughter, Martha, in July 1891, as well as a fourth child, Henry Clay Frick, Jr., who died in infancy the following summer.) To a banker friend, Frick confided that buying pictures gave him "more real pleasure than anything I have ever engaged in, outside business."

   In December 1899 Frick resigned definitively from Carnegie Steel Co., Ltd.—at issue was the price at which he was obliged to sell coke to the parent company—and requested that Carnegie buy him out. The following year witnessed the painful separation of these two titans of industry, with Frick suing Carnegie and gaining a settlement of $15 million. (In 1901 the Carnegie Company would be reorganized into the United States Steel Corporation, under J. P. Morgan's directorship, and Frick would serve on its board.) Although active on the boards of several railroad companies—his

6   Frick bought Johannes Vermeer's *Girl Interrupted at Her Music*, 1660, from Knoedler & Company in 1901.
Of thirty-six paintings by Vermeer, The Frick Collection has three, all purchased by the museum's founder.
The Frick Collection, New York.

first biographer claimed that he was "the largest individual railway stockholder in the world"—Frick
no longer had reason to remain in Pittsburgh. His profile as a collector was also changing: he bought
his first Rembrandt (*Portrait of a Young Artist*, now attributed to Rembrandt's studio) in 1899 and his
first Vermeer (*Girl Interrupted at Her Music* [fig. 6]) two years later. Gradually but decisively, Frick's
interests were turning away from modern art toward the old masters, particularly seventeenth-century
Dutch and Flemish landscapes and portraits and eighteenth-century British portraiture, so much
in vogue among collectors on both sides of the Atlantic at the turn of the century. When Mary
and Bernard Berenson, the American art critic and connoisseur of Italian art, visited Pittsburgh
in January 1904, Frick was informed that they desired "more particularly to see your pictures
than anything else."

7   Théobald Chartran, *Portrait of Henry Clay Frick*, 1896. Frick Art and Historical Center.

8   Eagle Rock, the Frick residence at Pride's Crossing, Massachusetts.

2. The Move East

The year 1905 was a watershed one for Frick (fig. 7) and his family. Having for some years rented a summer house at Pride's Crossing on Boston's North Shore, in 1902 Frick acquired three parcels of land on Hale Street overlooking the Atlantic (but with limited right of way to the ocean). He hired the Boston architects Arthur Little and Herbert W. C. Browne to design a 104-room brick mansion (fig. 8) and Cottier and Company to furnish it. Eagle Rock took three years to build, and Frick was determined that the place "be kept as simple as possible" (although there were silver-plated plumbing fixtures in each bathroom) and claimed to care not at all "whether it would be approved by Messrs McKim, Mead, and White, Messrs Carrère and Hastings, or Mrs. Edith Wharton." To Little, he insisted that the interior finishes be kept "severely simple," and that "while everything in

9   William H. Vanderbilt's Art Gallery at 640 Fifth Avenue, c. 1880.

connection with the house [should be] made of the best materials, we want it severely plain." These terms—and the manner in which they were voiced—will reappear in Frick's dealings with the architect and decorators of his New York home.

Despite his insistence on simplicity, it was into one of New York's most ornate dwellings that Frick and his family moved in the autumn of 1905. William H. Vanderbilt's neo-Grec brownstone at 640 Fifth Avenue (on the west side of the avenue, at 52nd Street) had been built and decorated by the Herter Brothers between 1879 and 1882 (fig. 9). Since 1896 it had been occupied by Vanderbilt's youngest son, George Washington (1862–1914), who had placed his father's collection on long-term loan at The Metropolitan Museum of Art and who, after some efforts at modernizing

10   Exterior of the William H. Vanderbilt residence, 640 Fifth Avenue, c. 1880.

the house, had embarked on the creation of Biltmore, a massive estate in Asheville, North Carolina. Vanderbilt *fils* leased his father's house to Frick for ten years at an annual rent of $50,000, and Frick seems initially not to have been daunted by the move into what Edith Wharton had referred to as this "Thermopylae of bad taste," with its balconied window projections, elaborately carved entablatures, and opulent architectural detailing (fig. 10). (As a young man, Frick had acquired Strahan's four-volume *Mr. Vanderbilt's House and Collection* and had hung framed prints of Vanderbilt's pictures at Clayton.) Although Frick and his family seem to have loved the long summers at Eagle Rock—to which many of his pictures were transported in steel-lined trains each season (figs. 11, 12)—the somewhat old-fashioned and oppressive opulence of the Vanderbilt mansion may have worn on them.

11, 12　　George Romney's *Henrietta, Countess of*
　　　　　Warwick and Her Children, 1787–89 (left),
　　　　　and workmen at Pride's Crossing moving
　　　　　the painting, about 1908.

13　　Charles Carstairs, 1928.

Such, at least, is the implication of a comment made in August 1912 by Charles Carstairs (1865–1928) (fig. 13), the head of Knoedler's London office and the dealer with whom Frick was on the closest terms. Congratulating Frick on engaging Hastings to build him a home, Carstairs wondered why it had taken him so long, particularly since "all the family will now take a greater pleasure in spending part of the year in New York." Ironically, Frick resided considerably longer at 640 Fifth Avenue than at 1 East 70th Street (ten years as opposed to four). One can't help thinking that Frick's dislike of excessive ornament and polychromy in interior decoration, and his desire for simplicity in general, were confirmed by his protracted experience as Vanderbilt's tenant.

3. East 70th Street

In December 1906, just over a year after settling in New York, Frick acquired the Lenox Library building and site on Fifth Avenue between 70th and 71st streets (200 feet along the avenue, 125 feet into the block) for $2,250,000 (figs. 14, 15). Four months later he added an additional parcel of land running some 50 feet east through the block, at a cost of $600,000. On 18 December 1906 *The New York Times*, which reported regularly on these transactions, claimed that it was Frick's intention "to build a home which shall rival, if not outclass, the Carnegie home, situated a mile further up Fifth

14   The Lenox Library, Fifth Avenue, east side from 70th to 71st streets, 1905.

15   View of the back of the Lenox Library showing the field between the library and Madison Avenue, c. 1880.

Avenue." More accurately, it also noted that Frick would not be able to take title to his latest
acquisition until the "new Public Library at Fifth Avenue and 42nd Street has been completed."
(The firm of Carrère and Hastings had been awarded the commission in 1897, and the New York
Public Library would be dedicated in 1911.)

For the dour and eccentric book collector James Lenox (1800–1880), Richard Morris Hunt
had built a neo-Renaissance château in gray granite, which was completed in the mid-1870s. The
building also housed Lenox's collection of paintings, to which the public had access on written appli-
cation, but the library, with its limited opening times and unwelcoming admittance, was chiefly known
as a "select resort for bibliomaniacs." In the decade after Lenox's death there had been some

modernization of the building, but—even after the decision had been taken to amalgamate the various benefactions into a new public library on 42nd Street—the heirs of his estate had maintained the founder's restrictions on the property, which remained limited to library use. (This was one reason why the New-York Historical Society had declined to acquire the site.) As a result, residential development along the south side of East 71st Street and the north side of East 70th Street had been severely curtailed, and Frick now engaged in long and delicate negotiations to persuade the Lenox heirs to sign the necessary releases so that building could begin (fig. 16).

Seventieth and Fifth was certainly a prestigious address, but in 1877 Henry James could still speak of the Upper East Side as

> *a region where the extension of the city began to assume a theoretic air, where poplars grew beside the pavement (where there was one) . . . and where pigs and chickens disported themselves in the gutter. These elements of rural picturesqueness have now wholly departed from New York street scenery; but they were to be found within the memory of middle aged persons in quarters which would blush now to be reminded of them* [Washington Square].

Pigs and chickens would indeed have been a distant memory when Frick's house was being built, and in December 1913 the *Times* devoted a long illustrated article to the expansion of private homes north of 59th Street, from Fifth to Park avenues, claiming that "in the past eighteen months, more plans have been filed for expensive private homes in this locality than has been the case for several preceding years." Lenox Hill was the most favored, and the most highly developed, "probably because it is several blocks nearer the social life of the city."

For his Fifth Avenue home, Frick had initially approached the Chicago architect Daniel H. Burnham (1846–1912), whose firm specialized in high-rise office buildings and had been responsible for the World's Columbian Exposition in Chicago and the Frick Building in Pittsburgh (among others) as well as the Flatiron Building in New York. Frick was in no great hurry to get started. He first mentions the project to Burnham in a letter of 29 June 1908, asking him if he "was east in the near future" to "run up here for a day or two" to "talk about that Lenox Library site." Intrigued, Burnham made a

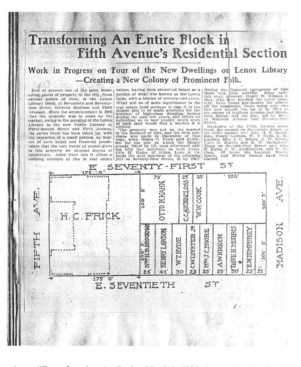

16   "Transforming An Entire Block in Fifth Avenue's Residential Section," article from unknown source.

point of studying domestic architecture in Europe in the winter of 1908 and reported to Frick in February 1909 that "he now felt up to your proposed job on the Lenox Library site." Considering both Stafford House and Bridgewater House in London as models—even if "very inferior in treatment to the sort I have in mind"—Burnham assured Frick that "my whole heart is in the thing; the building ought to distinguish your name for ever."

Only after the New York Public Library opened its doors in May 1911 was there any urgency in Frick and Burnham's discussions, yet somewhat perversely, Frick now directed his attention to a proposed addition to Eagle Rock, his home in Pride's Crossing. Fellow collectors P.A.B. Widener (1834–1915) and Benjamin Altman (1840–1913) were contacted for the dimensions of their picture galleries; Burnham and his contractor were urged to study the recently constructed Walters Art Gallery in Baltimore. Plans for a picture gallery at Pride's Crossing were drawn up by December 1911, and Frick seems to have shown them immediately to Widener (fig. 17), a Philadelphia collector, fellow director of the US Steel Corporation, and an active client of Knoedler's, whose taste in old masters and nineteenth-century paintings very much resembled Frick's own. (Widener's collection was housed at Lynnewood Hall, in Elkins Park, outside Philadelphia: an imposing neoclassical mansion designed by Horace Trumbauer between 1898 and 1901.) Widener apparently informed Frick "that he would no more think of retaining [Burnham] for a picture gallery than he would retaining anyone else for a great building," and this was enough to settle the matter, much to Burnham's chagrin.

Just as significantly, Thomas Hastings (1860–1929) (fig. 18) was now available for new projects. In April 1910 Hastings had been commissioned to design a gallery for Knoedler & Company at 556–558 Fifth Avenue (at West 46th Street), six blocks away from Frick's home. This discreet six-story palazzo (fig. 19), completed the same month as the Public Library, was inaugurated in January 1912 with an exhibition to which Frick lent several of his major works. Carstairs was on very good terms with Hastings (the architect addressed him as "my dear brother" and "my dear Grandpa"), and in early February 1912 brought him to the Vanderbilt house to consult on minor changes to the hanging of Frick's Barbizon pictures. On 7 February, Carstairs breathlessly informed Frick—away on a family holiday in Egypt—that he and Hastings had already had "several meetings," which had resulted in a dozen plans for the new house. Thanks to Widener and Carstairs, Frick had secured the services of New York's leading Beaux-Arts practitioner and the buoyant defender of academic classicism.

Hastings was an architect who attached great importance to the floor plan of a building. He noted that "the plan should be thoroughly studied and practically finished before the architect has more than a vague idea of the design of the exterior of the building." As such, he may have been

17   John Singer Sargent,
      Peter A. B. Widener, 1902.
      National Gallery of Art,
      Washington, D.C.,
      Widener Collection.

18   Thomas Hastings.

19   Knoedler & Company at 556–558 Fifth Avenue, with flags commemorating the Allied victory in World War I, 1918.

poorly served by Frick's constitutional reticence and a tendency to have others communicate his instructions for him. Frick's "curator" and secretary, James Howard Bridge (1858–1939), left a vivid account of the early relationship between client and architect: Hastings would go and see Frick and talk until he became nervous. "When I stop talking he gazes at me in silence in the most disconcerting way. Then I make a few more remarks, which are always received in silence; and when I come away, I am exhausted of all nervous energy." Frick seems not to have informed Hastings that the house would one day function as a museum; Bridge confirmed that he had deliberately "limited his understanding of what was required." Thus Hastings's initial plans for a monumental block recalling any number of Italian Renaissance palaces (figs. 20, 21, 22), built square around a central courtyard, with the entrance porch on 71st Street and a long gallery for pictures on the east side of the court, utterly failed to please.

20   Attributed to Thomas Hastings, design for the proposed Frick residence, c. 1912.

SEVENTIETH STREET ELEVATION
SCALE ⅛ INCH TO ONE FOOT

21   Attributed to Thomas Hastings, 70th Street elevation for the proposed Frick residence, c. 1912.

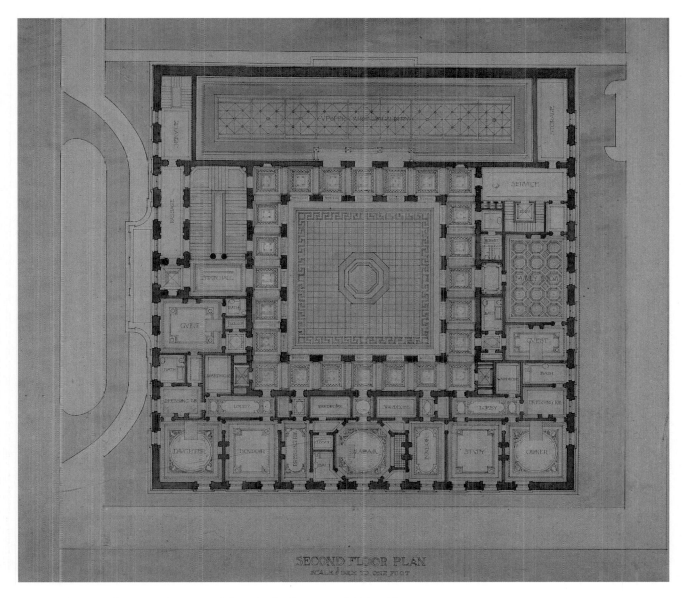

22   Attributed to Thomas Hastings, second-floor plan for the proposed Frick residence, c. 1912.

23   Thomas Hastings, south elevation, 70th Street, February 1913.

4. The House Emerges

By April 1912 Hastings had revised his concept. Carstairs informed Knoedler that Frick now "loved" the plan; by early June Hastings's drawings were sufficiently advanced for Widener to be consulted (he too gave his approval); and on 23 July Frick wrote to Carstairs—"My dear Charlie"—that the model of his new house, transported to Pride's Crossing, was the object of "unstinted praise." With Frick's earlier admonition for a house "kept simple and conservative in every way," Hastings designed a low-lying neoclassical Indiana limestone building in three blocks set back seventy-five feet from Fifth Avenue (figs. 23, 24). The front façade, with eleven windows on two floors and an attic story, looked onto a garden with Fifth Avenue beyond. It was anchored by a central portico, three windows wide, set off by four two-story Ionic pilasters and fronted by low, wide steps (fig. 25). As has recently been observed, this was a surprisingly subversive decision for a new Manhattan residence, since Hastings's design rejected the by now universal custom of building to the edge of the grid and erecting a

24   Thomas Hastings, north elevation, 71st Street, February 1913.

balustrade close to the property line. This section of the house, an early example of the Louis XVI revival, seems to have been inspired by the court-side façade of Cherpitel's Hôtel du Châtelet in Paris, built in 1770. To the north, the more baroque Gallery wing (fig. 26)—with its coupled columns, pavilion-loggia, and façade of seven pilaster bays on 71st Street (fig. 27)—evoked Louis XIV's Grand Trianon from the late seventeenth century. The third block of the house contained the Entrance on East 70th Street connected to a short wing, two stories high, with two windows on the Fifth Avenue Garden side. (*The New York Times* remarked on the lack of symmetry between the south wing and the Gallery wing to the north.) Set some way back from the street, a pair of elaborate wrought-iron gates (fig. 28) led to a porte-cochère and barrel vault resting on paired Tuscan columns (fig. 29), with the interior courtyard beyond (fig. 30). The rear of the house, facing into a court that was accessible by driveways from both 70th and 71st streets, was considered "perhaps the finest exterior of all."

25   View from Fifth Avenue. Photograph published in *Architecture*, November 1914.

26   Loggia and Gallery. Photograph published in *Architecture*, November 1914.

27   71st Street façade. Photograph published in *Architecture*, November 1914.

28   Main Entrance at 70th Street with gates by John Williams. Photograph published in *Architecture*, November 1914.

29   Main Entrance with open gates and porte-cochère, 1927.

30   View of interior courtyard.

31   Loggia at end of Gallery wing with neo-Renaissance carved motifs.

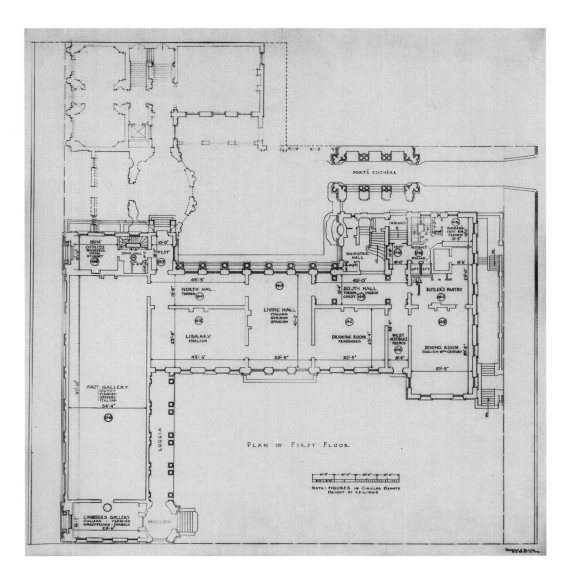

32   Thomas Hastings, ground-floor plan, 1916.

Notably restrained in its exterior ornamentation, the building's end pavilions and portes-cochères were surmounted by elaborately sculpted pediments, and the Loggia at the Gallery wing was carved with neo-Renaissance motifs (fig. 31).

For the ground floor of the interior—in which guests were customarily received and entertained on the grandest scale—Hastings proposed a distinctive dogleg axial plan, with the central axis intersecting the ones at each end at a 90-degree angle (fig. 32). Entering through the Vestibule at East 70th Street (fig. 33), the visitor ascended through the foyer toward the South Hall, anchored

33   Vestibule and Entrance Hall, 1927.

34   Main Staircase from the South Hall, 1927.

by the Stair Hall at right (fig. 34). Here, a second axis led toward the Gallery, passing from the South Hall (fig. 35) to the North Hall and uninterrupted by the central Living Hall (fig. 36). The halls acted as a sort of corridor for the public rooms, which consisted of a Dining Room, Drawing Room (later the Fragonard Room), Living Hall, and Library—each with views onto the Fifth Avenue Garden. There was neither music room nor ballroom at 1 East 70th Street. For music, Frick installed a beloved Aeolian organ in the Stair Hall, so that music could be heard at dinner. Although he was rumored to have paid $100,000 for an early-seventeenth-century organ, built in Nuremberg, he had in fact commissioned the Aeolian Company for a Pipe Organ, Opus 1263, at a cost of $40,000 (it was ordered on 15 July 1913 and in place by the following April). The gilded organ console, in an alcove at the foot of the stairs, was designed by White Allom to Hastings's design (fig. 37). The arched organ case above the landing was decorated with spiral colonnettes of Verona marble (fig. 38), its gilt figures inspired by Luca della Robbia's *Singing Gallery* for the organ loft of Florence Cathedral.

35   South Hall, 1927.

36   Walter Gay, *The Living Hall*, Frick residence, 1926.
Frick Art and Historical Center.

37   White Allom & Co., drawing for the
     organ console at the foot of the
     Main Staircase, c. 1913–14.

38   Detail of the organ case.

In place of a ballroom, the picture Gallery occupied the most magisterial space in the house: it was 100 feet long, 35 feet wide (fig. 39). In keeping with Hastings's country house designs, the staircase assumed a rather modest position in the overall plan; hallways expressed the pattern of movement within the building; and the walls of the square or rectangular rooms were not breached by bay windows or niches. The second floor comprised the family's private quarters and guest rooms. Staff and service areas occupied the third floor, the basement, and the subbasement below.

In August 1912 Hastings and his wife traveled to England with photographs of the model for Carstairs's inspection. Hastings also sought inspiration for the interiors of the house. He "was awfully keen and is visiting a great number of the important English country houses" (Carstairs took him to Roehampton and Hampton Court). Back in New York, under the supervision of D. B. Kinch, Frick's able superintendent of buildings, who had relocated from Pittsburgh for the project, the clearing of the site could finally begin, and by the end of October the Lenox Library had been dismantled and removed. Hastings's final plans and blueprints were drawn up in December 1912, and in January 1913 *The New York Times* estimated construction costs at between $2 million and $3 million. Journalists clearly had access to Hastings's plans, as an accurate description of the ground-floor rooms (including their dimensions) appeared in print on 5 January 1913. At this stage, the specifications also called for "an inner garden at the rear of the dwelling" and a "large fountain and sunken garden with a pool 60 feet long," southwest of the Fifth Avenue Garden (neither was built). The *Times* concluded "that the effect of the whole structure and the Gallery is one of general spaciousness"—an assessment that must have resonated with Frick.

He may have been less pleased when he reviewed Hastings's "Specifications for the Special Finish of Principal Rooms," submitted to him in March 1913. Among the suggestions that most certainly caught his eye—and which he rejected—were a polychrome frieze for his room at the west end of the Gallery (now the Enamels Room), inspired by the painted decoration at Knole in Kent; an ornamented and painted plaster ceiling for the Living Hall, based on the Long Gallery at Aston Hall, Birmingham; and a paneled walnut ceiling, "gold and colored," for his second-floor sitting room. At this point, the English decorator Sir Charles Carrick Allom (1865–1947) (fig. 40), who had recently redesigned the Balcony Room at Buckingham Palace for George V, made a successful pitch for the

39   West Gallery in 1927, looking east, with Velázquez's *King Philip IV of Spain*, 1644, in the center of the end wall. Frick purchased this painting from Knoedler & Company in 1911.

40   Sir Charles Allom, c. 1930.

ground-floor rooms. As the founder of White Allom, with a New York branch on East 52nd Street, Allom was fairly often in Manhattan and may well have been encouraged to offer his services to Frick by Knoedler and Carstairs. (He was certainly not put forward by Joseph Duveen, who, as Helen Frick noted many years later, at this stage "had nothing to do with the furnishing of the house.") Praising the plan of Frick's city house—"so exceptional and so fine"—Allom assured Frick that he could not "think of a great house with any aggressive ornamentation. The great point is the placing of all its ornamentation in such parts of the scheme as will ensure with certainty that nothing prevents the eye from traveling always to your works of art, whether picture or otherwise." As an example, "in no cases should great elaboration of ceilings be attempted, for their height is insufficient to place them out of the line of vision when the pictures are under consideration." This must have been music to Frick's ears.

41   West Gallery in 1927, looking west, with Paolo Veronese's *Wisdom and Strength* and *Virtue and Vice,* c. 1565, on the end wall.

5. The House and Its Interiors

Allom's thoughtful suggestions for each ground-floor room indicate that he had studied Hastings's model (or photographs of it) with the greatest attention. It was his opinion that the cove in the Library should be reduced in scale; that pilasters were not needed in the Gallery; that the central window in Mr. Frick's room overlooking Fifth Avenue never be allowed to interfere with the Veroneses when the Gallery doors were open (figs. 41, 42); and that the circle and garland motifs should be omitted from the Dining Room ceiling. All of these modifications were accepted, with Frick whole-heartedly in support of Allom's efforts to simplify and reduce ornament. One cable from Frick to Allom reads: "Please see that ceilings are almost plain; Hastings favoring too much carving. Please impress upon him my earnest desire to avoid anything elaborate." For his part, Hastings accepted Allom's participation with fairly good grace and in May 1913 traveled to London for a second time so that the two men could review the changes in each room. It is also clear that throughout the process Frick relied on Carstairs to settle any disagreements and to promote the case for "simplicity." A cable from Frick in early June 1913 reads: "Carstairs. Won't you please keep in touch with Allom. Hastings's ideas of decoration do not appeal to me."

42   Paolo Veronese, *Wisdom and Strength*, c. 1565.
The Frick Collection, New York.

43   Library of The Frick Collection, 1927. The British paintings seen here are, from the left, Sir Joshua Reynolds's *Selina, Lady Skipwith*, 1787; John Constable's *Salisbury Cathedral from the Bishop's Garden*, 1826; and Reynolds's *Elizabeth, Lady Taylor*, c. 1780. On the wall at the right, above the fireplace, is William Hogarth's *Miss Mary Edwards*, 1742.

If Frick demanded restraint of his architect and decorator—"We desire a comfortable, well-arranged house, simple, in good taste, and not ostentatious"—he did not hesitate to have them use the finest materials available. Thus, while he amended Hastings's initial specifications of March 1913, which called for Botticino or Rosato marble for the walls and columns in the Halls—he preferred leaving the stonework exposed—he accepted the use of these marbles in the entrance Foyer and Vestibule and approved laying the floors of the Foyer and Halls with Touraine marble. Austrian oak was designated for the floors of the Gallery and Mr. Frick's sitting room upstairs. As we have seen, Allom and Hastings might disagree over the treatment of the ceilings, with Hastings proposing the "very beautiful ceiling" from the Admiralty Building for the Dining Room, and that from Aston Hall,

44   Dining Room, 1927. John Hoppner's *The Ladies Sarah and Catherine Bligh*, c. 1790, is above the fireplace, and George Romney's *Charlotte, Lady Milnes*, 1788–92, is on the right.

Birmingham, for the Living Hall (neither was acceptable to Allom), but both men understood from the beginning that more than anything else Frick wanted paneled rooms to set off his paintings. As Hastings put it to Allom in a letter of 30 April 1913, "Do not fail to realize that we want as much space for the pictures as possible, and that all the paneling has been studied with this in view." For the Library, Allom proposed "a strong steady oak room of William and Mary character, with simple plain panels as background for pictures" (fig. 43). In the Dining Room, Georgian in design, the panels were to be "quite plain" to receive the full-length portraits "without picture frames" that Hastings had wanted to build into the woodwork itself (a decision that Frick wisely reversed when he hung his framed Gainsboroughs and Van Dycks in this room) (fig. 44). For the Drawing Room—the future

45   Main Staircase and balustrade.

46 Richard Cattermole, *The King's Staircase, Hampton Court* (detail), 1817–20, watercolor after Jean Tijou's staircase at Hampton Court.

47 Detail of iron balustrade, Main Staircase.

Fragonard Room—Allom envisaged paneling painted soft blue, with gilt moldings, evocative of the "classical Louis XVI style so frequently found in the best English houses." He was confident that, with judicious toning of the gilded ornament, "the inequality of the size of the pictures [in this room] would be less pronounced." (Shortly afterward, Mrs. Frick would suggest covering the walls in rose silk.)

The one detail over which Allom and Hastings did not argue was the wrought-iron balustrade for the Main Staircase (fig. 45), inspired by the Dean's Staircase at Saint Paul's Cathedral, London, designed by Jean Tijou (fl. 1689–1711), which had much impressed Hastings on one of his visits to London (he would also have seen Tijou's stairway at Hampton Court [fig. 46]). In commending this to Frick in early March 1913, while modifying (or rejecting) every other proposal that Hastings had presented for the interiors, Allom assured his client that the balustrade "may be the only ornate work in the house" (fig. 47). By the end of May each man would have agreed with Allom's assessment that

48   Construction of the Frick residence, looking northwest from the corner of Fifth Avenue and East 70th Street, 2 April 1913.

"the plan . . . is going to give Mr. Frick exactly what he wants: an extremely refined background for his works of art, all the details concentrated in the architectural features, and no reduction in the quality of the materials used, or the workmanship put into it."

While the niceties of ornament and wall treatment were being worked out in letters circulating between various parties in London and New York, progress on the site itself at 1 East 70th Street was rapid, with construction during the summer and autumn of 1913 running ahead of schedule (fig. 48). Kinch was confident that the house would be ready for furnishing by April 1914; he boasted to Frick's bookkeeper that they had not worked one hour of overtime and reported to Frick that Hastings had been "amazed" at the progress when he visited in July (fig. 49). (Hastings was less pleased when he saw them plastering in September, because the "men were so far ahead of the architects" [fig. 50].) Frick shared his superintendent's enthusiasm and informed Carstairs in October that

49   Construction of the Frick residence, aerial view looking west, 2 July 1913.

"the new home is making splendid progress: the windows are being put in, the plastering well under way, and everything seems to be working out well" (fig. 51). By November full-scale models for five pediments created by Piccirilli Brothers, who had carved the familiar lions *Patience* and *Fortitude* at the entrance to Hastings's Public Library, were delivered to the studios of the other sculptors engaged on the project. Sherry Edmundson Fry (1879–1966) executed the pediment over the porte-cochère (fig. 52), for which Audrey Marie Munson (1891–1996) had posed: dubbed "Miss Manhattan," she was the city's leading model for public statuary (fig. 53). Attilio Piccirilli (1866–1945) was responsible for the two pediments on the 71st Street façade, representing *Orpheus* and *Sculpture*. In January 1914 specifications were drawn up for the wrought-iron gateways and grilles to be provided by John Williams and Samuel Yellin (fig. 54). The exterior of the house was nearing completion.

50   Construction of the Frick residence, southwest wall of the Gallery and Loggia, 10 September 1913.

51   Construction of the Frick residence interior of the Gallery, 2 October 1913.

52   Pediment sculpted by Sherry Fry on the porte-cochère, 1933.

53   Audrey Marie Munson served as the model for numerous public sculptures, including the one carved by Daniel Chester French that is now in front of the Brooklyn Museum.

54   Entrance Hall gates by Samuel Yellin.

55   Elsie de Wolfe in her home at 123 East 55th Street, New York. From *The House in Good Taste*, 1913.

6. Upstairs (and Some) Downstairs:
Elsie de Wolfe and Furnishing 1 East 70th Street

On 27 January 1914 the former actress and much-heralded decorator of the Colony Club, Elsie de Wolfe (1865–1950), breathlessly solicited Frick for a share in the furnishing of his house (fig. 55). "How proud and pleased I should be to help in ever so small a way in such a splendid dwelling. Even one room I should gladly do . . . I am especially good at the fitting up and *comfort* of women's rooms, the intimate little tricks that no mere man, however clever he may be, can ever know." Such was the bantering, coquettish tone that would characterize much of de Wolfe's future correspondence with Frick—something that he would never have tolerated in his dealings with Carstairs or Allom—but for the moment her letter remained unanswered. At this stage, Frick seems to have been content with Allom as his decorator.

It should also be remembered that, while Frick had large residences in New York and on Boston's North Shore to furnish—and called on Duveen Brothers and Knoedler, among others, to assist—he had shown little interest in integrating items of first-rate decorative art into any of his homes; unlike Huntington, Morgan, Widener, or Altman, he was not in the market for tapestry, furniture, ceramics, or enamels. The French dealer René Gimpel remembered Knoedler telling him soon after he arrived in New York (in the early 1900s) that Frick "would never buy an antique piece of furniture or art object, and his home was arranged in the worst possible taste." On 2 April 1913, three days after the death of J. P. Morgan ("the great friend is no more") (fig. 56), "Uncle Henry" Duveen encouraged his nephew, Joseph Duveen (1869–1939) (see fig. 66), to proceed carefully with Frick—who had as yet purchased only a handful of old masters from the firm, in addition to reproduction furniture. "In offering objects to

56   John Pierpont Morgan.

Mr. Frick for his new home, you should not start out with things of enormous price for him, as he is not accustomed to the idea of Objects of Art of great value."

Two incidents may have prompted Frick to reconsider the role that the decorative arts (and French eighteenth-century art in general) would play in furnishing 1 East 70th Street. On 18 February 1914 The Metropolitan Museum of Art inaugurated the Loan Exhibition of the J. Pierpont Morgan Collection. Frick was among the 8,000 guests in attendance and, when the lights suddenly went out, would have witnessed the faintly comical sight of men and women in formal attire guiding their way with flashlights. As the *Times* reported, "The fact that so many persons in evening dress not

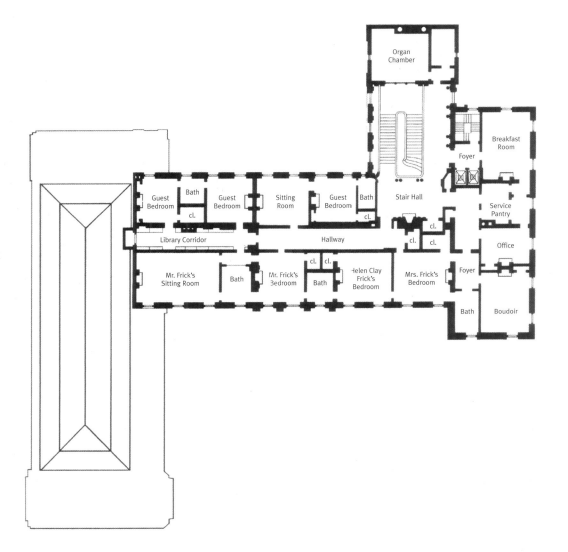

57   Richard Marchand, second-floor plan of The Frick Collection, 2005.

58   Henry Clay Frick's bedroom, 1927.

connected officially with the Museum should be carrying flashlights caused nearly as much surprise as the sudden darkness itself." This extraordinarily popular exhibition, the first American "blockbuster," would run for more than two years, closing on 28 May 1916. Some 4,100 works of art were on view in the new galleries designed by McKim, Mead & White. Gallery Nineteen, for example, was devoted to Fragonard's Progress of Love series, displayed, as the donor had wished, "in an exact reproduction of the room in which they were hung in Prince's Gate" in London. Thanks to Morgan's son, the original cornice, windows, doors, and paneling—designed by the Parisian decorators Carlhian and Beaumetz—were available for the installation.

59   Adelaide Frick's bedroom, 1927.

60   Adelaide Frick's bathroom, 1927.

While New York was honoring the Museum's former president (and Frick's long-standing business associate) on 6 March 1914, Frick's landlord at 640 Fifth Avenue died unexpectedly in Washington of a botched appendectomy. George Washington Vanderbilt's New York house now passed to his eldest nephew, Cornelius Vanderbilt III, who had been disinherited by his father for having married a wealthy society belle. The new owners were eager to take occupancy in October, and Frick—who was now aiming for "all to be in place" by mid-September—may have decided on the services of a second decorator to speed the process.

By mid-March Frick had hired de Wolfe to furnish four bedrooms and the housekeeper's room on the third floor and nearly all of the family rooms on the second floor (fig. 57)—seven bedrooms (figs. 58, 59), bathrooms (fig 60), Mrs. Frick's boudoir, and Miss Frick's library—but not the breakfast room or his sitting room (these were Allom's). On the ground floor, de Wolfe was allowed to do the ladies' reception room at the entrance to the house and a second reception room east of the Gallery that would later become Frick's office (fig. 61). There would be considerable jockeying between de Wolfe and Allom over Frick's study (fig. 62)—where de Wolfe would ultimately prevail—but on 25 March 1914 she submitted her first estimate of $10,384 for curtains for all the above-mentioned rooms. Clearly, at this stage Frick's attitude toward the decorative arts had undergone no radical reevaluation.

Frick's visit to London and Paris in the spring of 1914 marked a decisive stage in this regard. At the end of April Frick lunched at Lansdowne House with Victor Cavendish, ninth Duke of Devonshire (1868–1938), who remembered him as "a nice old man and very intelligent." A few days later, or 2 May, he was invited to Cavendish's country estate at Chatsworth, where—in addition to works by Memling and Rembrandt—he was most taken by a large suite of Gobelins tapestry furniture, which he intended for the Drawing Room at 1 East 70th Street. Cavendish, who had just succeeded to the dukedom and faced death duties of over £500,000, was inclined to sell something from the collection. The tapestry seating furniture (whose coverings were then considered to be from the Beauvais manufactory) consisted of eight fauteuils, two large canapés (fig. 63), and a fire screen. Frick acquired them for £40,400 ($202,000) and had them sent to Paris for restoration by Fry, Forest and Maus at 14 boulevard Malesherbes.

By mid-May Frick was staying at the Bristol in Paris, de Wolfe having arranged for him to see furniture from the collection of Sir John Murray Scott (1847–1912)—inherited from the widow of the founder of The Wallace Collection—in his former house on the rue Lafitte. The dealer Jacques

Seligmann (1858–1923)—whose firm, incidentally, had been responsible for the packing and shipping of Morgan's collection to New York in 1912–13—had acquired the entire contents of the rue Lafitte house, sight unseen, from Scott's beneficiary, Victoria, Lady Sackville (1864–1936), for a purported $2,000,000. Seligmann remembered Frick arriving "straight from the golf-course, dressed in plus fours and a plaid cap" and being "not at all disconcerted by the untidiness, the junkshop atmosphere of the cluttered rooms." (Frick would be back in London by the time the collection was moved to Seligmann's elegant gallery on the rue Saint-Dominique for public viewing.) Frick and de Wolfe chose a suite of nineteenth-century salon furniture, pairs of console tables and candelabra, and fine furniture by Carlin; a subsequent visit by de Wolfe to Seligmann's premises secured Riesener's beautiful *Writing Table* for $40,000, which Frick considered "very fine" (fig. 64). Between them de Wolfe and Seligmann found several more objects for Frick's consideration, but nothing more of significance was acquired. Still, in less than a month Frick had spent over $400,000 on furniture, far more than at any period in the past and comparable to the cost of Turner's *Harbor of Dieppe* and *Cologne: The Arrival of a Packet Boat*, purchased in 1914 from Knoedler for $320,000.

Frick returned home in early June and from Pride's Crossing reported to Elsie de Wolfe at her house, the Villa Trianon, in Versailles, that "great progress" had been made during his absence. Above all, he was "immensely pleased" with the Gallery—whose proportions he considered "just right"— and was hoping to move out of 640 Fifth Avenue by the middle of the month (the house would be handed over to "Nielly" Vanderbilt "much sooner than promised"). Frick never allowed his mounting enthusiasm to interfere with the supervision of accounts: on 9 June he came down very hard on Hastings for having an overrun on costs—figures for the house and grounds now stood at $1,700,000. However, two days later he was reassured by confirmation from Knoedler that some fifty-nine paintings had been safely moved from 640 Fifth to 1 East 70th Street. De Wolfe would have to sail for New York a month earlier than expected to supervise the installation of her rooms, he informed her on 11 June, since "the house will be completed surely by September 1st."

This was not to be. Frick's optimism for a speedy (and seamless) move was shattered by the outbreak of the First World War in August, and by his own illness—a severe bout of inflammatory rheumatism, which manifested itself at about the same time and kept him bedridden, at Pride's, until the middle of October. For Frick, initially, the war was at most a mild irritant (the family would come to follow the war's course with the utmost seriousness, with Helen in 1918 spending six months in France assisting in the repatriation of Belgian refugees). In a letter of 28 July 1914, he

61 Henry Clay Frick's office in 1927 with Gilbert Stuart's *George Washington*, 1795–96, above the
fireplace, James McNeill Whistler's *Harmony in Pink and Grey: Portrait of Lady Meux*, 1881–82, on
the left, and Whistler's *Symphony in Flesh Colour and Pink: Portrait of Mrs Frances Leyland*,
1871–74. This room was demolished during the conversion from a private residence to a museum.

62 Henry Clay Frick's study, 1927. Today this room is the office of the Chief Curator.

63   The canapé (top), with nineteenth-century tapestry covers, and the two fauteuils (bottom), with eighteenth-century tapestry covers woven by the Gobelins manufactory, were part of the salon furniture purchased by Frick from Victor Cavendish, ninth Duke of Devonshire, in 1914. The Frick Collection, New York.

regretted that "it looked so much like war . . . While I do not suppose it would seriously injure investments in this country, yet it is always expensive." Very quickly, however, the mass mobilization of working men and the requisitioning of raw materials for arms had an impact on the final stages of furnishing Frick's New York house. That Frick's timetable for completion would be disrupted—a thought that never seems to have occurred to him—was first indicated in an emotional letter from Elsie de Wolfe, whose Villa Trianon had been transformed into a hospital and officers' mess. Writing on 16 August, she could hardly describe the conditions in France: "Of course it will be a delay all along the line as to deliveries of the material. All the workers in the silk factories have gone to the war . . . But I hope with all my heart that the Germans will be whipped to a finish. It is entirely and absolutely their fault." With Allom, Frick was mired in an angry debate about the wall treatment for his Drawing Room, which was now to receive the tapestry furniture from Chatsworth, and which Mrs. Frick had apparently desired to see hung with rose silk. Allom disapproved of this color and strongly recommended paneling the room, since it was currently impossible to fabricate wall silks and curtains; Frick simply could not understand Allom's "inability to provide suitable materials." As to Allom's request for money on account—"In France, owing to the immense suffering and disturbance of business, it is only a kind and proper act to pay them with every possible speed"—Frick responded with a bluntness that bordered on insensitivity: "Am informed that there is no money due you. When there is you will be paid."

It was over the delay in carpets, curtains, wall hangings, locks, and light fixtures—all being fabricated in Europe to Allom's specifications—that Frick lost his temper with mounting vehemence (and wearisome regularity). The velvet for the Gallery's walls was ready to be shipped from Marseilles but did not leave port until 12 September, and one can sympathize with Frick's frustration at being prevented from hanging his pictures in the room he loved most. Many of the doors remained without locks well into November. This had been a particularly contentious issue, and Frick was not mollified by Allom's explanation that "the workmen in the metal trades" had been called up for "ammunition making." He cabled back on 29 October: "Simply outrageous unbusinesslike your dilatory manner completing contracts with me . . . War excuse absurd." Allom responded with a patient but defiant letter, noting that some of the locks "were fully one foot higher on the one side of the door than on the other" (fig. 65), and that since they were being made by hand, "with the locksmiths taken off to make rifles," there was "nothing in the world that we could have done." He assured Frick that one of his company's representatives was bringing five locks by hand and that carpets were being shipped

64   Jean-Henri Riesener, *Writing Table with Mahogany Veneer*, 1785–90. The Frick Collection, New York.

from Le Havre and Scotland in early November. When they were held up at the docks owing to congestion, Frick informed Allom on 6 November, "We are suffering the greatest inconvenience due to your want of foresight."

Ironically, it was in the November issue of *Architecture* that several photographs of Hastings's building appeared for the first time (see figs. 25–28), with the magazine reporting that "the most costly and sumptuous residence in the United States has just been turned over to its owner." Readers of this article could hardly surmise that Frick himself was deriving very little pleasure from his new home. Doors were still without locks, he explained to Allom on 18 November; only now were the backs being put into the fireplaces; his sitting room was without "a particle of furniture," there were no chandeliers in any room except the Living Hall, and the breakfast room was without a table. However, when on 21 November the Western Union Telegraph installed a stock ticker at 1 East 70th Street, certain essentials, at least, were finally in place.

7. Enter Duveen: Morgan's Collections at 1 East 70th Street

During the winter of 1914–15 Frick continued to fight with Allom: "I regret exceedingly that I did not give Miss de Wolfe the furnishing of my entire house, her work is practically done and absolutely satisfactory." He engaged in an acrimonious correspondence with Seligmann over shipping costs for the furniture acquired in May: on goods valued at $229,000, Frick steadfastly refused to pay transport charges of $1,700 and did no further business with Seligmann thereafter. And he scolded Elsie de Wolfe for her wayward accounting, revising the commission system on which she worked for him and insisting that in the future "any and all purchases" had to have his approval "in writing." Frick also witnessed the decline of his friend Widener, who remained incapacitated for the rest of the year. On 18 January 1915, Widener's youngest son, Joseph, informed him that "father's troubles are of a far more serious nature than rheumatism, and for this reason I hardly think it possible for him ever to be much better than he is now." (Widener died a week short of his eighty-first birthday in November 1915.)

But early in the New Year, developments of a more positive (and surprising) nature took place. In February 1915 Joseph Duveen (fig. 66) brokered the sale to Frick of the Fragonard panels then on display at the Metropolitan Museum for $1,250,000—by far Frick's most expensive acquisition to date and more than three times the price that Morgan had paid for them seventeen years earlier. Duveen Brothers made no profit on the transaction and also agreed to install these large wall paintings and overdoors in Frick's Drawing Room at cost. They undertook to supervise the modification of the room including all details of fabrication and lighting (fig. 67). This was an adroit move on the part of a dealer who had as yet played a relatively minor role in furnishing Frick with paintings or objects. As already noted, Frick's preferred dealer—and his good friend and golfing partner—was Charles Carstairs (see fig. 13), who since 1908 had been running Knoedler's office in London. Carstairs was intimately involved in the planning and construction of the house at 1 East 70th Street, and he and Frick remained in regular touch regarding pictures on the market. "There is no-one in whose judgment of the beautiful I have more confidence in than in yours," Frick noted in a letter of July 1908. Sincere sentiment, if slightly awkward syntax—and the only time he confided such heartfelt praise to writing.

In an interview with the *New York Herald* in December 1912, given while Morgan was still alive, the dealer Seligmann had noted that the Fragonard panels were among the objects that had cost the

66   Count Adolfo Felice Müller-Ury, *Portrait of Sir Joseph Duveen*, 1923. Private collection, New York.

67   The Fragonard Room featuring The Progress of Love panels, c. 1773.

financier the most, and that he could easily sell for twice or three times the price he had paid for them. While this had, indeed, proved to be the case, Duveen's decision to offer them to Frick at cost was part of a hugely ambitious, if somewhat risky project. In April 1915 he enlisted the services of A. Decour et Cie on the rue François Ier—which had recently installed Huet's suite of large pastoral paintings in comte Moïse de Camondo's mansion (the present Musée Nissim de Camondo)—to prepare a maquette of the new Fragonard Room at 1 East 70th Street. Duveen imposed Sir Charles Allom as a go-between with Decour (whom Frick considered "a very clever man") and had his brother Louis from the Paris office monitor progress week by week. In the sometimes daily telegrams between Paris and New York, Frick was given the code name "Maurice." Fabrication of the paneling of the new Fragonard Room began in June for completion in October 1915, when the family returned to New York from Pride's Crossing. Here Duveen's projections were wildly optimistic. For all Frick's hectoring that the room "be completely fixed here by November 1st at the very latest," it would not be ready until May 1916. "Maurice's" growing impatience was the subject of several communiqués.

Joseph Duveen's motives were clearly spelled out in a telegram of 12 June 1915 to his brother Louis: "The quicker done the better for us because enable us place more things in room." He intended

68   *Famille verte* female figures, Qing dynasty (1644–1912).

the Fragonard Room and, indeed, the rest of the house to serve as the setting for the finest objects from Morgan's collection and, beyond that, for objects from Duveen Brothers' stock. On 6 July Joseph rejected the initial design for the chimneypiece in the Fragonard Room because it was large enough neither for the room nor for the bust and candelabra from Morgan's collection that he wished to place on it. The following day he made his position even clearer. Louis was always to be present whenever Allom came to review work at Decour's, because "Everything depends upon this. For we repeat if room wonderful success our business next year with Maurice will be fabulous." His prediction turned out to be exactly right.

69   Giovanni Bellini, *St. Francis in the Desert*, c. 1480. Purchased by Frick in 1915, this is one of the few religious works in the Collection. The Frick Collection, New York.

70   Martial Reymond, *Apollo and the Muses*, second half of the sixteenth century. The Frick Collection, New York.

Duveen's confidence in his new client had already been confirmed when, in March 1915, the finest of Morgan's Chinese porcelains were sent to 1 East 70th Street and placed in the various ground-floor rooms and halls For a collector who had instructed Elsie de Wolfe not to pay more than $2,500 for eight candlesticks from Phillips, and who rejected a silver inkstand of 1720 as too expensive at $3,750, the prices that Frick was now willing to pay for *famille noire* Hawthorn vases, blue-and-white ginger jars, and *famille verte* female figures (fig. 68) simply beggar belief. Four pairs of *famille rose* ovoid jars and two bowls, destined for the Drawing Room, were priced at $261,000. The two female figures on stands, which were placed in the Living Hall and have remained there ever since, cost $130,000—just $40,000 less than Bellini's *St. Francis in the Desert* (fig. 69), acquired on 30 April for the same room. In early June 1915 Frick would contract to pay Duveen $1,391,600 for the group of Chinese porcelains, in monthly installments of $100,000.

The next month Duveen established four new accounts for Frick: Morgan Porcelain, Morgan Furniture, Porcelain, and Furniture. In addition, within a year Duveen would sell him forty enamels (fig. 70) from the Morgan Collection as well as Morgan's superb collection of small Renaissance and Baroque bronzes (fig. 71)—some of which, mounted on casters, Frick apparently delighted in seeing revolve on the low bookcases on which they were displayed. In addition to works for the Fragonard Room, Frick had purchased outstanding examples of Morgan's eighteenth-century French furniture and sculpture—Lieutaud's *Longcase Regulator Clock*, Riesener's *Commode* and *Secrétaire* (fig. 72) for Marie-Antoinette, and Clodion's *Zephyrus and Flora* (fig. 73). On 21 June 1916 Duveen presented Frick with a bill for all works consigned from the Morgan collection and acquired to date: not including the Fragonard Room, this amounted to $4,696,000. All but $500,000 was paid for in common stock of the Atchison, Topeka and Santa Fe Railroad. Frick's investments might be said to have allowed him to purchase not only Rembrandts but the full range of sculpture and decorative arts.

It was in the late spring of 1915 that Frick entertained at 1 East 70th Street for the first time, giving formal dinners for twenty-six men—a sign that his house was finally presentable. Alongside dinners for the president and board members of the US Steel Corporation, Frick also invited a mix of collectors, industrialists, and men in the "art world" (Hastings, Carstairs, Knoedler, and Duveen were all in attendance in April and May 1915). The rancor and bitterness of the previous winter seem largely to have been forgotten, with Frick positively jovial as he took Hastings to task for having made him pay too much for the construction of the house ("very artistic men are generally very poor business men"). He concluded his letter to Hastings of 2 June 1915: "We are enjoying it, and there are many features for which we are indebted to you. I think it is a great monument to you, but it is only because I restrained you from excessive ornamentation." Two weeks later he honored Hastings with a "Complimentary Dinner," which moved the architect to write that he was "proud to have had anything to do with the mere housing of such beautiful music and pictures . . . It means everything to me to have had so many artists see my work inside the house and better understand the general scheme." Among those in attendance on the evening of 17 June was the forty-two-year-old architect John Russell Pope, who would play a pivotal role in the transformation of 1 East 70th Street into The Frick Collection.

71   This fifteenth-century bronze lamp was crafted by the Paduan bronze sculptor Andrea Briosco, called Riccio, and purchased by Frick from
      Duveen Brothers in 1916. The Frick Collection, New York.

72 This *secrétaire* was signed and dated by Jean-Henri Riesener. It was designed for Marie Antoinette, as was the pendant *commode* also in The Frick Collection. Probably made in the mid-1780s, the piece was remodeled by Riesener in 1790. The Frick Collection, New York.

73   Claude Michel, called Clodion, *Zephyrus and Flora*, 1799. The Frick Collection, New York.

8. Frick's Final Years: A Proposed Expansion and the Last Acquisitions

In the early summer of 1915 there was still much to be done at 1 East 70th Street. Decour's model for the Fragonard Room had just been approved, White Allom was called in to improve ventilation in the Gallery, and Elsie de Wolfe was busy with Mrs. Frick's bedroom and boudoir on the second floor. In the midst of all this, on 24 June 1915 Frick executed his will and formalized the decision he had arrived at some years earlier to leave the house and its contents to the public, "For the purpose of encouraging and developing the study of the fine arts, and of advancing the general knowledge of kindred subjects."

74   Adelaide Frick's boudoir, 1927. This room now serves as the office of the Director.

75   Current view of the Boucher Room.

Inspired, perhaps, by the success of the Morgan exhibition at the Metropolitan Museum, and secure in the knowledge that, thanks to Duveen, Morgan's finest objects were his for the asking, Frick laid the foundations for a "public gallery . . . to which the entire public shall forever have access."

In making this bequest, Frick moved well beyond his original requirement for "a small house with plenty of light and air," a shift in purpose that is reflected in his later acquisitions. Within a year, the range of the objects in his house would be comparable in price and importance to that of his pictures. And the house itself was being modified in significant ways to display the expanding collection. By May 1916 the Drawing Room would be transformed into the Fragonard Room (see fig. 67); that same month, Mrs. Frick's boudoir (fig. 74) would provide the origins of the Boucher Room (fig. 75); and in March 1917 Mr. Frick's office would be remodeled to display

76   Enamels Room, 1927.

Morgan's Limoges enamels (fig. 76). It was not that Frick had in any sense lost interest in old master paintings—on the contrary, superb works by Titian, Hals, Vermeer, and Gainsborough entered the collection in the last years of his life. Rather, his tastes had broadened to include sculpture, furniture, and porcelains. And for the first time, eighteenth-century French painting became of interest to him.

The evolution of Frick's taste was accompanied by a subtle shift in his relationship to Knoedler, Duveen, and the market in general. Whereas he had once warned de Wolfe that most art dealers were "robbers," he now found himself increasingly beholden to Duveen for works of the highest quality.

Carstairs, with whom he remained on the best of terms and who would be one of the pallbearers at Frick's funeral, could not have been unaware of the gradual ascendancy of the house of Duveen. He expressed his irritation with these changing priorities to Knoedler in a letter of July 1915. Referring to what he perceived as Frick's "moratorium" on purchasing—something he had first brought to his partner's attention the previous autumn—Carstairs noted, "There is no chance to conclude any business with him. He seems to be interested in getting the house fixed, and the business will have to wait."

Duveen's business with Frick, by contrast, had never been better. Between March and July 1915 he placed Morgan objects in various rooms in 1 East 70th Street; in May 1916 Morgan's bronzes and Limoges enamels were brought to the house following the close of the exhibition at the Metropolitan Museum. Most galling of all for Carstairs must have been Duveen's success in selling Frick Boucher's panels of the Arts and Sciences, acquired from Maurice Kann's collection in the autumn of 1909 and held as stock since that time. In December 1915 Carstairs had offered Frick a composite group of six mythologies by Boucher. They were, he claimed, "more beautiful than any of the Bouchers in the Wallace Collection . . . and in my thirty-one years of business experience, I have never seen such Bouchers for sale." Frick had declined three of the most significant works and acquired *Poetry, Drawing,* and *Girl with Roses*—the more modest of the group—for $75,000 in May 1916. (Knoedler eventually sold *Cupid and the Three Graces* to the Portuguese collector Calouste Gulbenkian the following year.) That same month, Duveen sold Boucher's Arts and Sciences series to Frick for the considerable sum of $500,000 (the paintings are now attributed to Boucher and his studio) (fig. 77).

Boucher's panels were installed in Mrs. Frick's second-floor boudoir, whose ceilings had to be raised to accommodate them. Hastings drew up plans and supervised the contractors, and Duveen had Carlhian and Company in Paris prepare the paneling and provide parquet flooring for the room. In September 1916 Duveen assured Mrs. Frick that he was on the "look out" for appropriate furnishings. Even though the room was ready by November 1916—and Duveen complimented Hastings, referring to him as "my dear Lorenzo de Medici," for finishing it so quickly—well into the following year the dealer continued to search for "comfortable furniture . . . so that the room may be displayed in all its perfect beauty." Among the works he placed there were Louis-Noel Malle's *Writing Table,* the *Commode with Pictorial Marquetry* attributed to Gilbert, and the set of Sèvres *Pots-Pourris-Myrte with Flemish Scenes and Landscapes* (fig. 78); these were finally acquired in May 1918. In precisely the same way as he had done with the Fragonard Room, Duveen used the transformation of Mrs. Frick's boudoir to sell Frick furniture, porcelain, and sculpture; this time, however, all the objects came from his own stock, rather than from the Morgan Collection.

77　It was long assumed that Madame de Pompadour, mistress of Louis XV and a great patron of the arts, commissioned the panels now in the Boucher Room for her château at Crécy. Today the Arts and Sciences series is believed to have been composed in the studio of her preferred painter, François Boucher, for an unknown patron. Pictured here are *Architecture* (top) and *Chemistry*, c. 1760. The Frick Collection, New York.

78　Sèvres Manufactory, *Pot-Pourri-Myrte with Flemish Scene and Landscape*, c. 1762. The Frick Collection, New York.

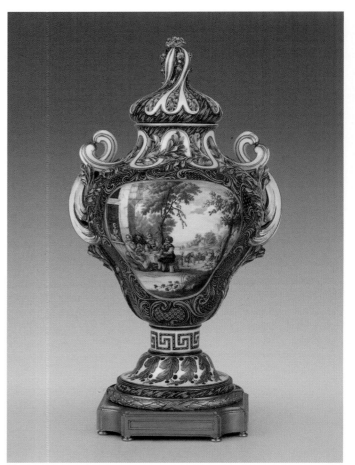

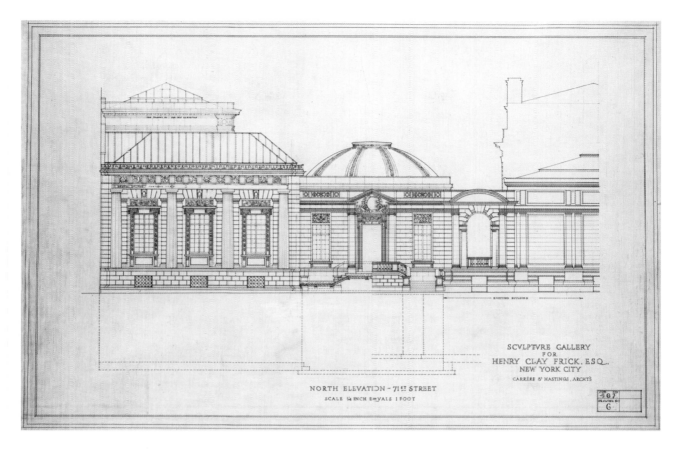

SCVLPTVRE GALLERY
FOR
HENRY CLAY FRICK, ESQ.
NEW YORK CITY
CARRÈRE & HASTINGS, ARCHTS

NORTH ELEVATION - 71ST STREET
SCALE ¼ INCH EQUALS 1 FOOT

79   Thomas Hastings, proposed sculpture gallery, north elevation, 71st Street, 1916.

Less than a year after taking possession of 1 East 70th Street, and three months after writing his will, on 29 September 1915 Frick authorized Hastings to draw up plans for an extension to the house. The architect was to design a sculpture gallery one and a half stories high in a block adjacent to the West Gallery, occupying the 50-foot plot at 6–8 East 71st Street that Frick had just purchased. Frick seems to have instructed Hastings to remain silent about this addition. It was only after *American Art News* published an article on "Mr. Frick's New Art Gallery" in March 1916 that Duveen seems to have got wind of the scheme. On 18 March he cabled Allom at his home in the suburbs of London: "See Frick today has bought property next door. Hastings finished designs, but your cooperation needed.' A few days later, Frick reminded Hastings that he was not to file any plans without his approval. He was assured "that none of us here even talk to outsiders about the Gallery."

Hastings's plans and sketches, on which he worked throughout 1916, extended the façade on East 71st Street by six bays (fig. 79). A single-story entrance block, its pedimented doorway flanked by windows on either side, contained an entrance hall with an oval room beyond. Next to this was a

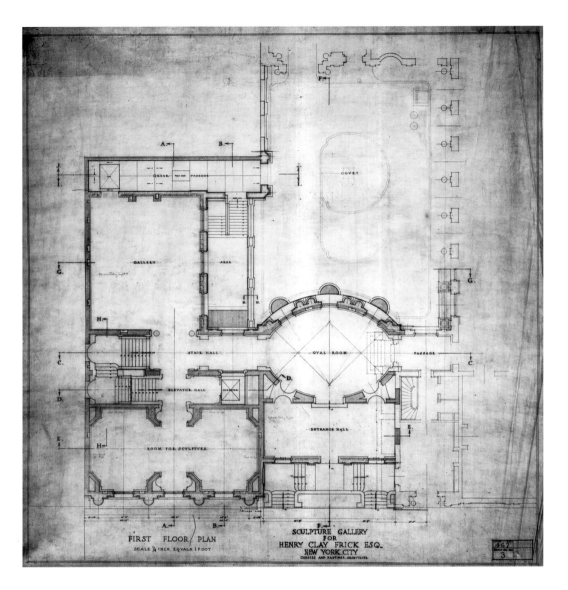

80   Thomas Hastings, proposed sculpture gallery, ground-floor plan.

three-bay wing, with imposing Doric columns and ornamented entablature, that housed a "Room for Sculpture" and a gallery (fig. 80). A sketch for the interior shows vaulted and pilastered rooms, with Baroque portrait sculptures on pedestals—one with a curious resemblance to Bernini's *Cardinal Richelieu*—and Carpeaux's *Ugolino and His Children* installed in a place of honor (fig. 81).

Given that Frick owned no works by Bernini or Carpeaux, one might ask how he intended to fill these rooms. Three magnificent bronzes acquired for $445,000 from Duveen in June 1916— Cattaneo's *Bust of a Jurist* (purchased as a portrait of Titian), Brandini's *Antonio Galli* (then attributed to

81   Thomas Hastings, proposed sculpture gallery, interior.

Jacopo Sansovino), and Jonghelinck's *Duke of Alba* (fig. 82)—doubtless provided the impetus for such an installation. But in the end, even with Duveen's best efforts, the lack of a substantial collection of gallery-scale statuary surely discouraged Frick from proceeding. In late October 1916 he received assurance from Hastings that the blueprints and drawings for "the proposed new addition" were almost completed. This time not only Carstairs and Allom but Duveen as well were expected to review and approve them. Over the winter months, however, Frick resisted pressure to award the contracts for the exterior of the building. "Would you not like to see the drawings?" ends a plaintive letter from Hastings, written on 13 December 1916; "I will gladly bring them to you at any time which you may suggest."

By mid-January 1917 Frick's change of mind seems to have been complete. He informed Hastings that, in view of the scarcity of labor and rising costs of construction, "I have decided to do nothing whatsoever towards the erection of the new building until times become normal and perhaps reasonable." On 27 April, in response to neighbors' complaints about "certain people making use of the lot on 71st Street," he asked Hastings to erect a fence around the vacant property. And there matters might have remained, except that with Frick having abandoned the proposed addition, Hastings quite reasonably sought to be remunerated for the work his office had undertaken. He waited almost fifteen months until he was launched on the Cunard Steamship Company building on Lower Broadway before bringing this up again in March 1918. Frick predictably requested a statement of the outstanding account and was much exercised when he received Hastings's "absurd bill" for $45,000. In an explosive letter of 18 March, Frick railed against Hastings's habitual extravagance—"The present house cost me thousands of dollars more than you estimated it would cost originally"; denied responsibility for the addition—"You rushed into this work largely on your own account"; and questioned Hastings's claim that his chief draftsmen had been "continuously employed" on these plans for nearly two years—"I do not know how many draftsmen you have continually employed from the time you mention, but their brain power must have been at a low ebb; they certainly were not overworking themselves." Hastings patiently reviewed the size and scope of the proposed addition—which, as he pointed out, covered not only the entire adjoining lot but also part of the present house's interior courtyard—and, as expected, in June 1918 Frick agreed to send him $20,000 on account, with the

82   Jacques Jonghelinck sculpted this bronze portrait bust of Don Fernando Alvarez de Toledo, third Duke of Alba, in 1571. Frick purchased the piece from Duveen Brothers in 1916. The Frick Collection, New York.

remainder to be paid only if he decided to abandon the project definitively. He hinted that there was still the remote possibility that he would undertake construction after all, but "not, of course, until after the war."

If Frick was cautious about expanding the site of his present home (and future museum), he showed no such reticence in adding to his collection in the last two years of his life. In negotiating terms for Duveen's bill of $2,196,479, submitted on May 1918, Frick reminded the dealer, "It is a serious question whether anyone should at this time invest so much money in works of art, but as I contemplate all this as a gift to the public, I feel somewhat justified in doing so." If we consider only the old masters that Frick acquired in 1918 and 1919, we find Duveen responsible for Hals's *Portrait of a Man* (then identified as the Dutch naval hero Admiral de Ruyter), Vermeer's *Mistress and Maid* (fig. 83), Gainsborough's *Mrs. Baker*, and Pater's *Procession of Italian Comedians* and *The Village Orchestra*. Duveen also placed Renaissance sculpture, Baroque bronzes, Limoges enamels, and eighteenth-century furniture at 1 East 70th Street. Accounts show that he was prepared to accept a modest profit—if any—on many of these masterpieces. The Hals was sold at cost; for the Vermeer, Duveen's firm acted only as an intermediary in gaining a license under the Trading with the Enemy Act so that *Mistress and Maid* could be acquired from a Berlin industrialist. Only Gainsborough's *Mrs. Baker* brought Duveen a more healthy return, but even here his markup was unspectacular. Frick was billed $300,000 for a painting that had cost the dealer $254,000. Duveen had his eyes trained resolutely on the future, since it was his habit to place works on long-time consignment at 1 East 70th Street, and rarely was he in any hurry to see them returned. During these last years, paintings by Andrea del Sarto, Titian, and Van Dyck and marble busts by Houdon were installed in the ground-floor rooms on approval, with Frick never pressed to come to a decision on whether or not to acquire them. Following an attack of ptomaine poisoning in November 1919 that would prove fatal, Frick seems to have been quite anxious that this consignment be returned to Duveen, lest possession be considered indication of an intention to acquire. On 29 November, three days before his death, works of art valued at $1,500,000 traveled the fourteen blocks south back to Duveen's premises at 720 Fifth Avenue.

83   Johannes Vermeer, *Mistress and Maid*, 1665–70. The Frick Collection, New York.

9. 1920–35: The First Frick Art Reference Library and the Creation of The Frick Collection

In accordance with Frick's instructions, within four months of his death The Frick Collection was officially incorporated and a group of hand-picked trustees appointed to its board. In addition to his widow and two children, there were nine members, including Horace Havemeyer, John D. Rockefeller Jr., and J. Horace Harding—Andrew Mellon and Junius Morgan joined the board in the early 1930s—each of whom was offered an honorarium of $50,000, "as an expression of my gratitude for his aid in carrying out a purpose which I have long cherished and which is very dear to me." On an estate valued at $150 million—of which the house and its contents at 1 East 70th Street constituted by far the greatest entity—only one-sixth went to Frick's family, with the remainder going to public and charitable institutions in New York, Pittsburgh, Princeton, and Cambridge, Massachusetts. *The New York Times* reported less than a week after his death that more than $117 million had been left in "gifts for the Public benefit . . . the largest single testamentary benefaction to public welfare ever made." Frick had made provision for his widow to remain at 1 East 70th Street for the rest of her life; at her death, the house and its collection would be turned into a museum, for which an endowment of $15 million had been established. As well as supporting building, maintenance, and operating costs, the interest was to be spent in adding works of art to the Collection.

The first project embarked on by the newly constituted board was to erect a library on the vacant lot at 6–8 East 71st Street. Frick's daughter, Helen Clay (1888–1984) (fig. 84), long interested in cataloguing her father's collection, had for some time been building an art history reference library, much of it housed, for lack of space, in the Bowling Alley (fig. 85) and Billiard Room (fig. 86) at 1 East 70th Street. On a visit to London in May 1920, after meeting the collector and bibliophile Robert Witt (1872–1952)—a trustee of the National Gallery, whose Library of Reproductions was bequeathed to the Courtauld Institute as the Witt Index—she was inspired to create a photographic archive that would document European and American paintings in public and private collections. To accommodate the reference library and photographic archive, in December 1922 the board approved a one-story building at 6–8 East 71st Street, across from the carriageway that led to the interior courtyard of 1 East 70th Street. Hastings's new design for

84 Helen Clay Frick, photograph by Henry Havelock Pierce, c. 1910. National Portrait Gallery, Smithsonian Institution, Washington, D.C. Gift of the Clayton Corporation, Pittsburgh.

85   Bowling Alley.

86   Billiard Room. 1933.

the Library derived from his plans for Frick's abandoned addition, which had become the property of the estate in January 1920 on payment of the outstanding balance of $25,360 (fig. 87).

Leaving the carriageway untouched (fig. 88), the Library occupied only the site previously intended for Frick's sculpture gallery—a three-bayed square pavilion of Indiana limestone (fig. 89). Hastings's revised drawings of February 1923 merely repeated the squat classical façade that he had designed six years earlier, with its weighty Doric columns and ornate mullions and pediments; he now placed the railed entrance at the northwest corner of the building. Its interiors decorated in Cape Cod colonial style, the first Frick Art Reference Library building opened to the public in June 1924, with a staff of a librarian and twenty assistants. *International Studio* marveled at "the celerity with which the resources are placed at the reader's disposal." If the Library's efficiency was "decidedly breathtaking," Helen Frick was less than happy with the building's construction. A litany of complaints is recorded, with Helen particularly enraged by the design of the front door stoop (fig. 90), so narrow that anyone standing there "ran the risk of being knocked down the steps each time the door was opened."

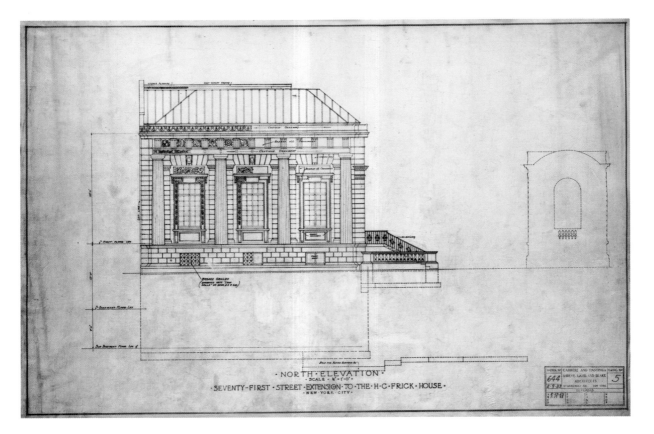

87   Thomas Hastings, north elevation, 71st Street extension, original Frick Art Reference Library, 1923.

88   Frick Art Reference Library, carriage driveway, and Henry Clay Frick's office, c. 1924–32.

89   View of the original Frick Art Reference Library, facing East 71st Street, c. 1924–32.

(As a remedy, the entrance door had to be opened in reverse.) Hastings's lack of attention to these issues also drew a rare rebuke from Adelaide Frick; by the summer of 1926 relations between Hastings and the Frick women were at their lowest ebb In a letter of 9 August, Helen informed him that "If a change should be made at any future time and the space be filled in between the house and the Library, as trustee of the Frick Collection, I would seriously oppose the engaging of your firm as architects." As Hastings died of a ruptured appendix in October 1929, Helen's determination not to use his services again would never be put to the test.

90　　Front door of the original Frick Art Reference Library, 6 East 71st Street, c. 1924–32.

92　　John Russell Pope.

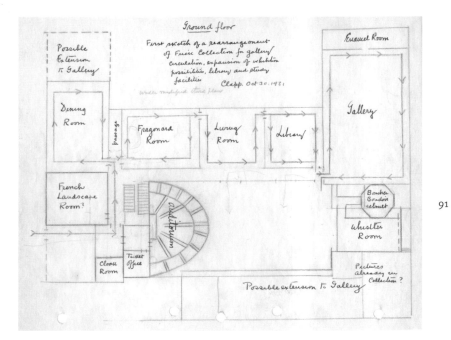

91　　Frederick Mortimer Clapp's "First sketch of a rearrangement of Frick Collection for gallery/circulation, expansion of exhibition possibilities, library and study facilities," 30 October 1931. Clapp was appointed organizing director of The Frick Collection in 1931 and oversaw the conversion of the residence into a public museum.

Helen's outburst confirms that thoughts for the future of The Frick Collection were never far from the family's mind. While Adelaide was alive and in occupancy at I East 70th Street, discussion centered on her daughter's desire to see the Library expand into more commodious quarters. A particularly acrimonious debate in April 1929 over plans for three additional floors to the building at 6–8 East 71st Street—drawn up at Helen's request by Walter Dabney Blair, architect of the McIntire Building, Charlottesville's first municipal library, and rejected by the board—give some insight into how the transformation of the house itself was envisaged at this time. In noting that his mother might decide to stop living at I East 70th Street before her death, Childs Frick (1883–1965) ventured that windows would have to be built into the walls adjacent to the North and South Halls—with the Fragonard Room completely reconfigured—so that visitors could view the rooms and their contents through doorways, without entering them. The notion of maintaining the downstairs reception rooms as a series of "period rooms," to which Helen Frick was resolutely opposed, would finally be abandoned in December 1931, on the joint recommendation of Paul Sachs of the Fogg Art Museum and Belle de Costa Greene of the Morgan Library.

That such eminent professionals had been brought in to give advice on installation and security barely three months after Mrs. Frick's death—she had died at Pride's Crossing in October 1931, aged seventy-two—suggests that the trustees wasted no time in beginning work on the transformation of the house. Already on 30 October 1931, Frederick Mortimer Clapp (1879–1969), a Pontormo specialist and former professor of art history at the University of Pittsburgh, who was appointed organizing director of The Frick Collection that year, presented the board with five different designs for the first and second floors of an enlarged museum (fig. 91). As a general principle, the "whole collection" was to be displayed on the ground floor "for the purposes of exhibition and study," with the second floor used "for demonstration and study." Frick's ground-floor office next to the West Gallery would become the "Boucher boudoir rebuilt"; adjacent to this octagonal room, a new rectangular gallery was to house the Whistlers. On the southern side of the courtyard Clapp proposed a French landscape room, a cloak room, and a demi-lune auditorium.

Two renowned architects were invited to submit plans for the new museum. Childs Frick's preference seems to have been for Delano and Aldrich, who had designed the original Walters Art Gallery in 1909, a building his father had much admired. The other candidate, promoted by Rockefeller, Mellon, and Duveen, was John Russell Pope (1873–1937) (fig. 92), like Hastings a product of the Beaux-Arts tradition and committed to maintaining and refining the classicism of a previous generation (by the time of his death, he was dubbed "the last of the Romans"). Although he was nearing

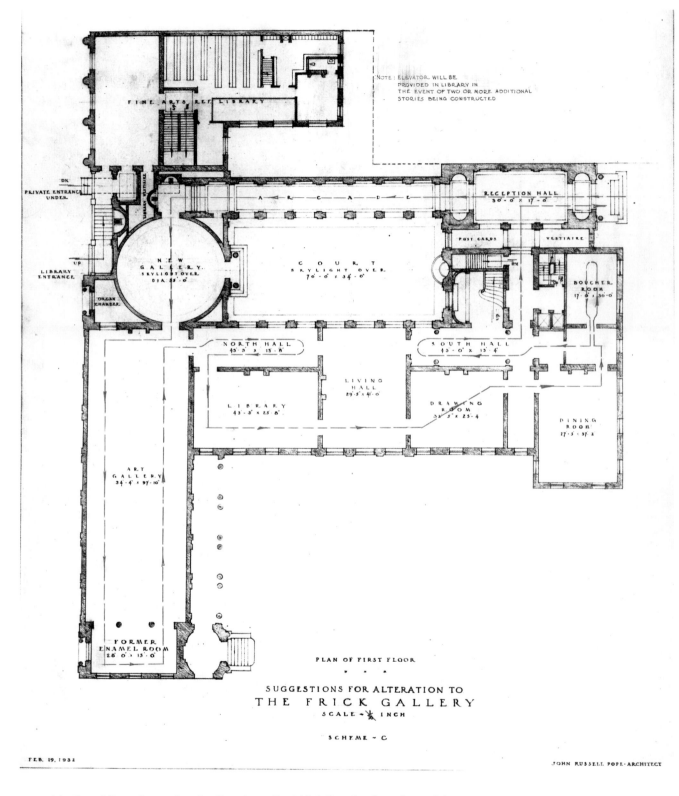

NOTE: ELEVATOR WILL BE
PROVIDED IN LIBRARY IN
THE EVENT OF TWO OR MORE ADDITIONAL
STORIES BEING CONSTRUCTED

FINE ARTS REF. LIBRARY

PRIVATE ENTRANCE
UNDER

LIBRARY VESTIBULE

RECEPTION HALL
30'-0" X 17'-0"

A   R   C   A   D   E

POST CARDS   VESTIAIRE

NEW
GALLERY.
SKYLIGHT OVER.
DIA. 55'-0"

COURT
SKYLIGHT OVER.
70'-0" X 34'-0"

UP   DN

BOUCHER
ROOM
17'-0" X 30'-0"

LIBRARY
ENTRANCE.

ORGAN
CHAMBER

UP

NORTH HALL
43'-3" X 13'-8"

SOUTH HALL
43'-0" X 13'-4"

UP

LIVING
HALL
29'-5" X 41'-0"

LIBRARY
43'-3" X 25'-8"

DRAWING
ROOM
32'-5" X 25'-4"

DINING
ROOM
27'-5" X 37'-2"

ART
GALLERY
34'-4" X 97'-10"

FORMER
ENAMEL ROOM
28'-0" X 15'-0"

PLAN OF FIRST FLOOR

SUGGESTIONS FOR ALTERATION TO
THE FRICK GALLERY
SCALE ⅛ INCH

SCHEME - C

FEB. 19, 1932

JOHN RUSSELL POPE · ARCHITECT

93   John Russell Pope, *Suggestions for Alteration to The Frick Gallery*, first-floor plan, 19 February 1932.

the end of a successful career, Pope was busier than ever with museums. He had worked on two additions for the Metropolitan Museum; was invited by Rockefeller in 1929 to submit designs for a museum of medieval art at the Cloisters (his withdrawal from which in January 1931 left him free to compete for the Frick project); and at Duveen's initiative designed the monumental gallery for modern sculpture at the Tate Gallery, as well as the gallery for the Parthenon marbles at the British Museum.

Pope proposed clearing the former courtyard and enclosing it under glass (fig. 93), thereby creating a Garden Court complete with palms, plants, and a sunken pool and fountain in the center (fig. 94). He also provided a new entrance on 70th Street by extending the façade over the former carriageway and relocating Hastings's porte-cochère as the doorway to the new museum (fig. 95). Fry's pediment, sculpted in 1913, now looked down on visitors as they crossed the threshold of the new museum. These ingenious solutions seem to have won Pope the commission in March 1932. At this stage, however, with Hastings's Library occupying the site at 6–8 East 71st Street, there could only be limited expansion north and east of the Garden Court. In building over the driveway at 71st Street and extending the West Gallery's façade by almost half its length, Pope gained sufficient room for only one new circular gallery, of admittedly generous proportions (see fig. 93). A breakthrough had occurred by the time he submitted a set of revised plans in August 1933. Pope now proposed demolishing Hastings's one-story Library, thereby allowing the Collection to expand into both the interior

94   An unicentified man with a model of the Garden Court fountain in Charles G. Peters's studio, Long Island City, New York.

courtyard and the adjoining plot at 6–8 East 71st Street (see fig. 111). The 71st Street façade was thus almost doubled in length, with Piccirilli's *Sculpture* pediment relocated from above the columned windows of Mr. Frick's former office to the fourteenth bay, where it now marked the end of Pope's extension (fig. 96). Connected to the Collection, a new Library, thirteen stories high (eleven of them above ground), would be built at 10 and 12 East 71st Street, the site of the former residences of James B. Clemens and Mrs. C. C. Auchincloss, purchased by the trustees in the winter of 1932. In April 1933 Pope's final plans and estimates for both the addition to the Collection and the new Library were submitted for the trustees' approval, with construction costs projected at $1,941,000. After approval in early May, building began in earnest (fig. 97). In less than a year, by April 1934,

95 Current entrance to the Collection on 70th Street with relocated pediment by Sherry Fry.

96   Remodeled façade of East 71st Street, 1948.

97   Construction of The Frick Collection, 16 April 1934 (showing Hastings's original library still standing).

Pope's Italianate Library, built of the same Indiana limestone as the house, was nearing completion; it would open to the public in January 1935. By the end of the year, the new Frick Collection was also ready, with seven hundred invited guests attending an inaugural reception on 11 December 1935. Massive rebuilding and new construction had been carried out with a speed and efficiency that would surely have impressed the founder.

Upon entering through the original porte-cochère, now relocated on 70th Street, visitors found themselves in a new rectangular Entrance Hall, which offered two routes into the collection. Turning west, they rejoined the original trajectory of the house, passing through the Vestibule into the South Hall, North Hall, and West Gallery beyond. Alternatively, visitors could continue north through the

98   John Russel Pope, sketch for proposed court and planting, April 1932.

99   Garden Court.

Entrance Hall into the newly created Garden Court (figs. 98, 99), with Pope's Oval Room (figs. 100, 101), East Gallery (fig. 102), and Music Room (figs. 103, 104) arrayed to the north and east. Everything was designed to disguise the transition from the original house to its modern additions: similar marbles, woods, and stone were used wherever possible, and the decoration of the Garden Court—with its paired Ionic columns and shields and cartouches—consciously evoked the classical vocabulary disseminated throughout the house. "It will be difficult for the viewer unfamiliar with the house as it stood three years ago to realize what tremendous changes have been wrought to make a handsome private dwelling into an efficient museum building," noted Alfred Frankfurter in *The Art News* on 14 December 1935.

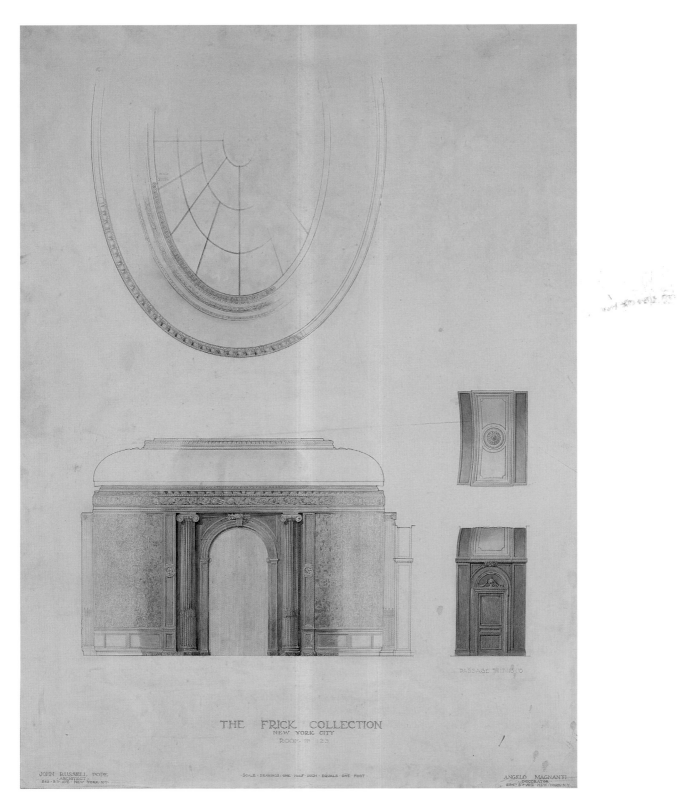

100   Angelo Magnanti for John Russell Pope, Oval Room elevation (detail), 1935.

101   Oval Room, 1935.

102   East Gallery, 1935.

103   Angelo Magnanti for John Russell Pope, Music Room elevation (detail), 1935.

104 Music Room, 1935.

Initially, at least, the Collection imposed a prescribed route on its visitors, leading them directly to the Oval Room—in which Frick's four Whistlers were installed around Velázquez's *King Philip IV of Spain* (fig. 105) (Houdon's *Diana* was not acquired until 1939)—and then to the East Gallery beyond (see fig. 102), from which beckoned Ingres's *Comtesse d'Haussonville* (fig. 106), acquired in 1927. Installation shots from this period show that both the paintings and furniture in these rooms were roped off, and from early accounts we know that the public was obliged to proceed through the original rooms between roped pathways. These restrictions were abandoned after the first year, in which more than 135,000 people visited the Collection. From January 1937 admission tickets were no longer required, the Collection was open on Sundays from 1 to 5, the velvet guide ropes were for the most part removed, and a preferred route was no longer prescribed. Slide lectures were given twice weekly, and from November 1938 concerts took place in the Music Room throughout the year (fig. 107).

105   Diego Rodríguez de Silva y Velázquez, *King Philip IV of Spain*, 1644. The Frick Collection, New York.

106   Jean-Auguste-Dominique Ingres, *Comtesse d'Haussonville*, 1845. Purchased by the Trustees of The Frick Collection in 1927. The Frick Collection, New York.

107   The Music Room during a concert in August 1997 featuring The Panocha Quartet.

Epilogue: Adding a Reception Hall and the 70th Street Garden

Just as Pope's additions to the Collection were intended to draw as little attention to themselves as possible—many visitors now naturally believe that Frick and his family had inhabited the entire space of the current museum—so was the Collection's development carefully monitored to be "in harmony" with the tastes and preferences of its founder. With one exception. As head of the board's Acquisition Committee until her resignation in January 1961, Helen Frick passionately encouraged the acquisition of works of the early Italian schools. Her father had shown very little interest in the Primitives, as they were then called. Apart from the fifteenth-century Burgundian *Pietà*, acquired on Roger Fry's advice in 1907 as an Antonello da Messina, and the magisterial *Deposition* by Gerard David (purchased in 1915), he seems not to have been moved by devotional painting from the early Renaissance (one reason for Berenson's dislike of him). His daughter, on the other hand, had genuine feeling for early Renaissance painting, as well as a good eye: the *Pietà* now ascribed to a follower of Konrad Witz that she acquired in 1926 (and donated to the Collection in 1981) is likely to have been the prototype for the Burgundian copy that Fry had imposed on her father. Thus, between 1924 and 1950 great paintings by Cimabue, Duccio (fig. 108), Filippo Lippi, and Piero della Francesca entered the Collection, and these were complemented by Piero's *Crucifixion* and busts by Verrocchio (fig. 109) and Laurana, bequeathed by former trustee John D. Rockefeller Jr. in 1961. (It was both poignant and ironic that their acceptance was to cause Helen such grief; she remained adamantly opposed to other collections infiltrating The Frick Collection.) In 1949 Helen had also prevailed on the trustees to deaccession a group of fine Post-Impressionist pictures, acquired between 1938 and 1940. Cézanne's *Chestnut Trees at Jas de Bouffan* (now in the Minneapolis Institute of Art), his *Dominique Aubert, the Artist's Uncle as a Monk* (The Metropolitan Museum of Art, New York), and Gauguin's *Tahitian Landscape* (Minneapolis Institute of Art) were each considered "discordant notes" in the context of the Collection. Henry Frick's interest in modern painting was decidedly not pursued. He had, after all, acquired outstanding works by Whistler, Manet, Degas, and Renoir—all at prices well below those of his old masters—and had even been intrigued by Cézanne's *Woman with a Rosary* (National Gallery, London), which he saw at the Armory exhibition in February–March 1913, where it was by far the most expensive work for sale. (He was put off by the asking price of $48,000.) Of the Collection's later acquisitions, only Monet's lyrical *Vétheuil in Winter* (fig. 110), acquired in 1941, evoked Frick's interest in the art of his own time.

108   Duccio di Buoninsegna, *The Temptation of Christ on the Mountain*, 1308–11. This panel was part of a series depicting scenes from the life of Christ on the double-sided *Maestà* altarpiece installed in the Duomo in Siena. The Frick Collection, New York.

109 Andrea del Verrocchio, *Bust of a Young Woman*, fifteenth century. The Frick Collection, New York.

110 Claude-Oscar Monet, *Vétheuil in Winter*, 1879. The Frick Collection, New York.

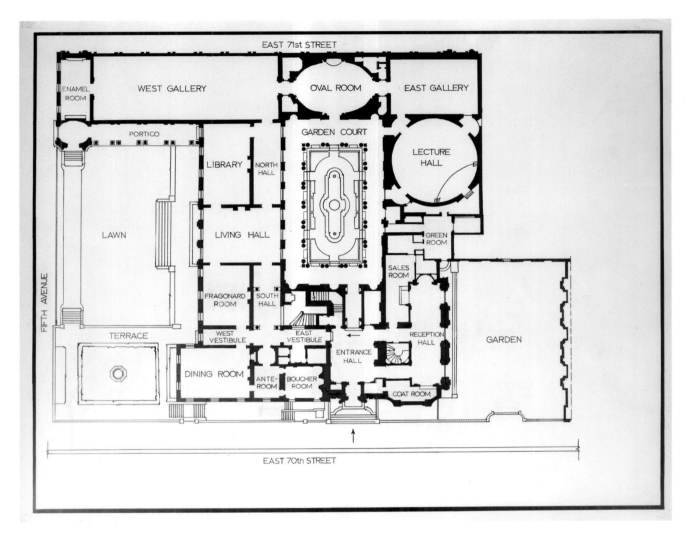

EAST 71st STREET

ENAMEL ROOM · WEST GALLERY · OVAL ROOM · EAST GALLERY

PORTICO · GARDEN COURT · LECTURE HALL

LIBRARY · NORTH HALL

LAWN · LIVING HALL · GREEN ROOM

SALES ROOM

FIFTH AVENUE

FRAGONARD ROOM · SOUTH HALL

RECEPTION HALL · GARDEN

WEST VESTIBULE · EAST VESTIBULE

TERRACE · ENTRANCE HALL

DINING ROOM · ANTE-ROOM · BOUCHER ROOM

COAT ROOM

EAST 70th STREET

111   Complete floor plan of The Frick Collection with 1977 additions, 29 July 1976.

   With considerable growth through purchase and acquisition well into the 1950s—since then, the Collection has continued to attract important gifts and to make occasional acquisitions by purchase—the trustees were also attentive to the possibilities of future expansion, buying the house at 9 East 70th Street in November 1940 and its neighbor at 7 East 70th Street in 1946, but having to wait until 1972 before the George Widener house at 5 East 70th Street became available. Now in possession of three contiguous townhouses on East 70th Street, the trustees initiated plans for a large wing and garden, which were approved by the Landmarks Preservation Commission on 6 July 1973. The architect John Barrington Bayley, working with Harry Van Dyke and G. Frederick Poehler, revised

112   Addition to The Frick Collection, 1977.

the initial specifications to reduce the addition to a small one-story pavilion, whose façade consciously emulated Louis XIV's Grand Trianon at Versailles (and echoed Hastings's colonnaded wing at the north of the property). The ground floor of this building housed a Reception Hall, Coat Room, and small Shop (fig. 111); its lower floors, intended as seminar and study rooms, were soon transformed into exhibition galleries. Construction on the 16,468-square-foot addition began on 23 May 1975; the new building, of the same Indiana limestone as the rest of the house, opened to the public in March 1977 (fig. 112). Paul Goldberger, writing in *The New York Times*, noted that this "seventeenth-century French style annex is so unthinkably out of fashion that it becomes in a strange way sort of daring."

113   Russell Page, photograph by Elliott Erwitt, 1976.

The most distinctive feature of this new addition was the 70th Street Garden designed by the Englishman Russell Page (1906–1985) (figs. 113, 114), at the entrance of which were placed John Williams's wrought-iron gates for the original porte-cochère. The gardens at 1 East 70th Street had enjoyed a somewhat checkered history. Thirteen thirty-year-old chestnut trees, replanted by Frick on the Fifth Avenue sidewalk in December 1913 and hailed as "one of the largest operations of the kind done in the city for many years," had soon perished because of leaking gas mains. Hastings and Frick abandoned their plans for a sunken garden on the Fifth Avenue façade, and for the new Frick Collection, Pope had merely envisaged lawns of grass planted with mulberry trees. On Rockefeller's recommendation, in July 1935 the Collection appointed Frederick Law Olmsted Jr. (1890–1957), son of the planner of Central Park, as garden designer for the new museum. For the Fifth Avenue

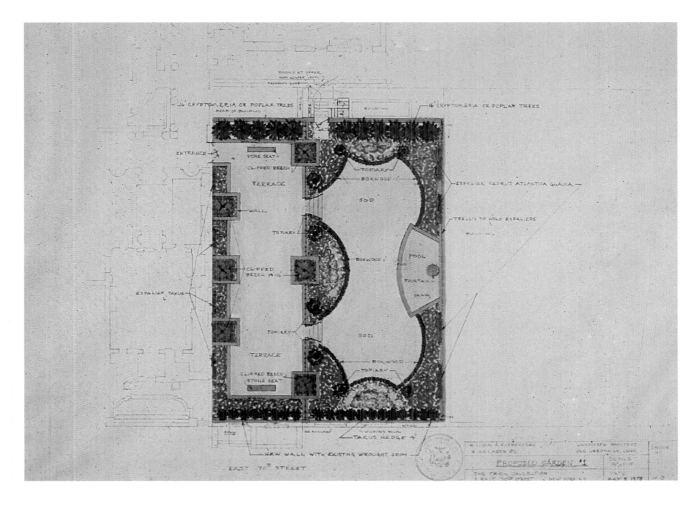

114   Drawing for the 70th Street Garden

115   Fifth Avenue Garden, showing Olmsted's privet hedges and the recently planted magnolia trees, 1939.

Garden, Olmsted proposed Hatfield yew hedges and in March 1939 oversaw the planting of three magnolias (two of which died within a year) (fig. 115). The star magnolia that survived the first planting was joined by two saucer magnolias, planted the following year. Their flowering each spring still constitutes one of the great pleasures of visiting The Frick Collection at that season (fig. 116).

For the first time then, in the 1975 addition, the Garden constituted a major element of the design. Page also recommended that the privet hedges on the Fifth Avenue Garden be replaced with flower beds and reshaped the magnolias by reducing their height and width (they are pruned every July to maintain their distinctive spreading form). With the support of Martha Frick Symington, one of Frick's four grandchildren and a former president of the Garden Club of America, Page was encouraged to design for the addition "a garden that will be alive with birds, that will display

116   Magnolias in the Fifth Avenue Garden today.

imaginative, first-class materials, that will be gay in Spring and Fall, cool and quiet in summer, and shining green and red in winter." He presented plans for a large rectangular reflecting pool, with paths of pea gravel; only his proposal for fountain jets along the east wall was rejected by the trustees. Trees were placed in December 1976 and the Garden unveiled the following spring. With its changing flowers, textures, and colors, Russell Page's 70th Street Garden was always intended to be experienced as a tableau, rather than to be entered (fig. 117). Best viewed from the Reception Hall by those inside the building, and from the street itself by those outside, it remains a patch of greenery and tranquillity in this most elegant part of the city and a fitting testimony to Frick's requirement that his New York house have "plenty of light and air."

117   Current view of the 70th Street Garden.

Select Bibliography

This aid for further reading has been ordered so that the most pertinent books and articles of general interest appear first. Topics include Henry Clay Frick and the Frick family, art in The Frick Collection, domestic house museums, art collectors contemporary with Frick, and collecting in the Gilded Age. Further readings, listed in accordance with the chapters of the text, follow.

Archival material used in this study was predominantly drawn from the institutional archives of The Frick Collection and the Frick family papers, located at the Frick Art Reference Library. Descriptions of selected holdings contained in the Frick archives may be found on The Frick Collection's Web site, *www.frick.org*.

General Reading

Ayres, William S. "The Domestic Museum in Manhattan: Major Private Art Installations in New York City, 1870–1920." Unpublished Ph.D. dissertation, University of Delaware, 1993.

Ballon, Hilary. *Mr Frick's Palace*. New York: The Frick Collection, 2009.

Bridge, James Howard. *Millionaires and Grub Street: Comrades and Contacts in the Last Half-Century*. New York: Brentano's, 1931.

The Frick Collection: An Illustrated Catalogue. Volumes I–IX. New York: Princeton University Press, 1968–2003. Contains entries for all works in the Collection.

The Frick Collection. Paris: Fondation BNP PARIBAS, 2011.

Munhall, Edgar, with Susan Grace Galassi, Ashley Thomas, and the Acoustiguide Corporation Staff. *The Frick Collection / A Tour*. New York: The Frick Collection in association with Scala Publishers, London, 1999.

Ossman, Laurie, and Heather Ewing. *Carrère & Hastings: The Masterworks*. Photography by Steven Brooke. New York: Rizzoli, October 2011.

Ryskamp, Charles, Bernice Davidson, Susan Grace Galassi, Edgar Munhall, and Nadia Tscherny. *Art in The Frick Collection. Paintings. Sculpture. Decorative Arts*. New York: Harry N. Abrams in association with The Frick Collection, 1996.

Sanger, Martha Frick Symington. *Henry Clay Frick. An Intimate Portrait*. New York, London, Paris: Abbeville Press, 1998.

———. *The Henry Clay Frick Houses. Architecture, Interiors, Landscapes in the Golden Era*. New York: The Monacelli Press, 2001.

Steffensen-Bruce, Ingrid A. *Marble Palaces, Temples of Art: Art Museums, Architecture, and American Culture, 1890–1930*. Lewisburg, PA: Bucknell University Press and London: Associated University Press, 1998.

Warren, Kenneth. *Triumphant Capitalism: Henry Clay Frick and the Industrial Transformation of America*. Pittsburgh: University of Pittsburgh Press, 1996.

Weisberg, Gabriel P., DeCourcy E. McIntosh, and Alison McQueen, eds. *Collecting in the Gilded Age. Art Patronage in Pittsburgh, 1890–1910*. Hanover, NH, and London: University Press of New England, 1997.

I. Origins in Pittsburgh

Brignano, Mary. *The Frick Art and Historical Center: The Art and Life of a Pittsburgh Family*. Pittsburgh: The Frick Art and Historical Center, 1993.

Sanger. *Henry Clay Frick: An Intimate Portrait.*

Warren, Kenneth. *Triumphant Capitalism.*

Weingartner, Fannia, ed. *Clayton: The Pittsburgh Home of Henry Clay Frick: Art and Furnishings.* Pittsburgh: University of Pittsburgh Press, 1988.

Weisberg et al. *Collecting in the Gilded Age.*

2. The Move East

Bridge. *Millionaires and Grub Street.*

Gray, Christopher. Research by Suzanne Braley. *New York Streetscapes: Tales of Manhattan's Significant Buildings and Landmarks.* New York: Harry N. Abrams, 2003.

Kathrens, Michael C. *Great Houses of New York: 1880–1930.* New York: Acanthus Press, 2005.

Tauranac, John. *Elegant New York: The Builders and the Buildings: 1885–1915.* New York: Abbeville Press, 1985.

3. East 70th Street

Bridge, James Howard. *Pictures in the Collection of Henry Clay Frick, at One East Seventieth Street, New York.* New York: Privately printed, undated.

Dain, Phyllis. *The New York Public Library: A History of Its Founding and Early Years.* New York: The New York Public Library, 1972.

Lydenberg, Harry Miller. *History of The New York Public Library.* New York: The New York Public Library, 1923.

"More Old Masters Added to the Widener Collection." *The New York Times,* 17 December 1911.

National Gallery of Art. *Paintings and Sculpture from the Widener Collection.* Washington, DC: Publications Fund, National Gallery of Art, 1948.

"The Private Home Centre Is Advancing Up Fifth Avenue." *The New York Times,* 7 December 1913.

4. The House Emerges

Blake, Curtis Channing. "The Architecture of Carrère and Hastings." Ph.D. dissertation, Columbia University, 1976.

Brooks, Diana. *Thomas Allom (1804–1872).* London: British Architectural Library, RIBA, 1998. (See, especially, the appendix on Sir Charles Allom.)

"Henry Clay Frick Residence, New York City: Thomas Hastings, Architect." *Architecture: The Professional Architectural Monthly,* November 1914, pp. 251–52, plates CXXV–CXXIX.

Thomas Hastings, Architect. Collected Writings Together with a Memoir. David Gray, ed. Boston: Houghton Mifflin Company, 1933.

Smith, Rollin. *The Aeolian Pipe Organ and Its Music.* Richmond, VA: The Organ Historical Society, n.d.

5. The House and Its Interiors

Andrews, Jack. *Samuel Yellin, Metalworker.* Ocean Pines, MD: SkipJack Press, 2000.

Lombardo, Josef Vincent. *Attilio Piccirilli: Life of an American Sculptor*. New York and Chicago: Pitman Publishing Corporation, 1944.

Rozas, Diane, and Anita Bourne Gottehrer. *American Venus: The Extraordinary Life of Audrey Munson, Model and Muse*. Los Angeles: Balcony Press, 1999.

Sanger. *The Henry Clay Frick Houses*.

Wattenmaker, Richard J. *Samuel Yellin in Context*. Flint, MI: Flint Institute of Arts, 1985.

6. Upstairs (and Some) Downstairs: Elsie de Wolfe and Furnishing 1 East 70th Street

Campbell, Nina, and Caroline Seebohm. *A Decorative Life*. New York: Panache Press, 1992.

De Wolfe, Elsie. *After All, by Elsie de Wolfe . . .* New York and London: Harper & Brothers, 1935.

Gimpel, René. *Journal d'un collectionneur marchand de tableaux*. Paris: Calmann-Lévy, 1963.

Munhall, Edgar. "Elsie de Wolfe. The American Pioneer Who Vanquished Victorian Gloom." *Architectural Digest*, January 2000, 149–51, 238–39.

Seligman, Germain. *Merchants of Art, 1880–1960: Eighty Years of Professional Collecting*. New York: Appleton-Century-Crofts, 1961.

Smith, Jane S. *Elsie de Wolfe: A Life in the High Style: The Elegant Life and Remarkable Career of Elsie de Wolfe, Lady Mendl*. New York: Atheneum, 1982.

Sparke, Penny. *Elsie de Wolfe: The Birth of Modern Interior Decoration*. New York: Acanthus Press, 2005.

7. Enter Duveen: Morgan's Collections at 1 East 70th Street

Bailey, Colin B. *Fragonard's Progress of Love at the Frick Collection*. New York and London: The Frick Collection in association with D Giles Limited, 2011.

Behrman, Samuel Nathaniel. *Duveen*. London: Hamilton, 1952.

Davidson, Bernice, with Edgar Munhall. *The Frick Collection: An Illustrated Catalogue. Volume II: French, Italian and Spanish Paintings*. New York: The Frick Collection, 1968.

Pope, John A., and Marcelle Brunet. *The Frick Collection: An Illustrated Catalogue. Volume VII: Oriental and French Porcelains*. New York: The Frick Collection, 1974.

Secrest, Meryle. *Duveen: A Life in Art*. New York: Knopf, 2004.

Verdier, Philippe, Maurice S. Dimand, and Kathryn C. Buhler. *The Frick Collection: An Illustrated Catalogue. Volume VIII: Enamels, Rugs and Silver*. New York: The Frick Collection, 1977.

8. Frick's Final Years: A Proposed Expansion and the Last Acquisitions

Ayres. "The Domestic Museum in Manhattan."

Pope-Hennessy, John, Anthony F. Radcliffe, and Terence W.I. Hodgkinson. *The Frick Collection: An Illustrated Catalogue. Volumes III and IV: Sculpture*. New York: The Frick Collection, 1970.

Ryskamp et al. *Art in The Frick Collection.*

Steffenden-Bruce. *Marble Palaces, Temples of Art.*

9. 1920–35: The First Frick Art Reference Library and the Creation of The Frick Collection

Bedford, Steven McLeod. *John Russell Pope.* Monticello, IL: Vance Bibliographies, 1982.

———. "Museums Designed by John Russell Pope." *Magazine Antiques,* 139, 1991, 750–63.

———. "The Architectural Career of John Russell Pope." Ph.D. dissertation, Columbia University, 1994.

———. *John Russell Pope: Architect of Empire.* New York: Rizzoli, 1998.

Knox, Katharine McCook. *The Story of the Frick Art Reference Library: The Early Years.* New York: The Frick Art Reference Library, 1979.

"Legacy of Beauty." The Frick Collection 1935. New York: The Frick Collection, 1995.

Reist, Inge. "Helen Clay Frick—Charting Her Own Course." In *Power Underestimated: American Women Art Collectors.* Edited by Inge Reist and Rosella Mamoli Zorzi. Venice: Marsilio Editori, 2011, 163–83.

Epilogue: Adding a Reception Hall and the 70th Street Garden

The Frick Collection: An Illustrated Catalogue. Volumes I–IX. Lee, Galen. "Gardens of The Frick Collection from Olmsted to Russell Page." Unpublished manuscript, 1997.

Munhall et al. *The Frick Collection/A Tour.*

Page, Russell. *The Education of a Gardener.* New York: Random House, 1962.

———. "The Shaping of a Garden." *House & Garden,* vol. 149, no. 7, 1977, 34, 36.

Photograph Credits

Photograph credits available to the authors and not otherwise provided in captions are as follows:

Courtesy of Acanthus Press: 10

Michael Bodycomb: 6, 11, 31, 38, 42, 45, 47, 63–65, 67–72, 75, 78, 82, 83, 85, 95, 99, 105, 106, 109, 110, 116, 117

Photo Corbis-Bettman: 40

Richard di Liberto: 73, 77, 108

Elliott Erwitt/Magnum Photos: 113

The Frick Collection/Frick Art Reference Library Archives: frontispiece, 1–3, 8, 12, 20–24, 29, 30, 32–35, 37, 39, 41, 43, 44, 48–52, 58–62, 74, 76, 79–81, 86–91, 93, 94, 96–98, 100–104, 111, 112, 115

Courtesy Knoedler & Company, New York: 13, 19

Clipping (undated, unsourced) from William B. May Company scrapbook. Courtesy of Christopher Gray: 16

© The Adolfo Müller-Ury Stiftung, Hospental, Switzerland. Photograph courtesy of Lawrence Steigrad Fine Arts: 66

© Museum of the City of New York: 15

Image © Board of Trustees, National Gallery of Art, Washington, D.C.: 17

Photography Collection, Miriam and Ira D. Wallach Division of Art, Prints and Photographs, The New York Public Library, Astor, Lenox and Tilden Foundations: 14 (photo by John P. Soule), 56 (photo by Pach Brothers)

The New York Public Library Archives, The New York Public Library, Astor, Lenox and Tilden Foundations: 18

The Royal Collection © 2006 Her Majesty Queen Elizabeth II: 46

Courtesy of Diane Rozas: 53

© Jack Vartoogian/FrontRowPhotos: 107

Elsie de Wolfe, *The House in Good Taste*, 1913: 55

Courtesy of Clare Yellin, Samuel Yellin Metalworkers: 54

Index

Note: Page numbers in *italics* are for illustrations. Index entries starting with numbers are filed as spelled (e.g., "70th Street Garden" is indexed as "seventieth").